Bombers, Rioters and Police Killers

Bombers, Rioters and Police Killers

Violent Crime and Disorder in Victorian Britain

Simon Webb

PEN & SWORD
HISTORY

First published in Great Britain in 2015 by
Pen & Sword History
an imprint of
Pen & Sword Books Ltd
47 Church Street
Barnsley
South Yorkshire
S70 2AS

ISBN 978 1 47382 718 9

Typeset in Ehrhardt by
Mac Style Ltd, Bridlington, East Yorkshire
Printed and bound in the UK by CPI Group (UK) Ltd,
Croydon, CRO 4YY

Pen & Sword Books Ltd incorporates the imprints of Pen & Sword
Archaeology, Atlas, Aviation, Battleground, Discovery, Family
History, History, Maritime, Military, Naval, Politics, Railways,
Select, Transport, True Crime, and Fiction, Frontline Books, Leo
Cooper, Praetorian Press, Seaforth Publishing and Wharncliffe.

For a complete list of Pen & Sword titles please contact
PEN & SWORD BOOKS LIMITED
47 Church Street, Barnsley, South Yorkshire, S70 2AS, England
E-mail: enquiries@pen-and-sword.co.uk
Website: www.pen-and-sword.co.uk

Contents

Introduction

I t is a curious and undeniable fact that many, perhaps most, people in the UK are likely to have gained more of their ideas about life in Victorian Britain from works of fiction than from actually studying history. The images and characters from Charles Dickens' novels, in particular, are likely to have seeped imperceptibly into our collective unconscious; shaping and moulding what we think we know about life in the nineteenth-century. It is hard to visualize London in the early part of Victoria's reign without being influenced, even subliminally, by thoughts of Fagin, the Artful Dodger and Mr Pickwick. Imagining a Victorian Christmas will almost inevitably conjure up the spirits of Bob Cratchit and Tiny Tim. Of course, Dickens is not the only author responsible for our vision of Victorian Britain. Think, for example, of governesses at that time and Jane Eyre springs unbidden into our minds.

This phenomenon, whereby we tend unwittingly to treat Victorian novels and their various adaptations on television and in cinema as being in some way an accurate mirror of the age which produced them, can give us a horribly distorted picture of the past. It leads a lot of us to see Britain in the nineteenth-century as a respectable, well-ordered and highly moral, if somewhat prudish and hypocritical, society; a time when this country was not plagued with undesirable modern scourges such as gun-toting criminals, terrorist bombers, mugging, gangs and riots. The expression 'Victorian Values' hints at this view of the nineteenth-century. Those were the days when there was respect for authority and children did as they were told; an era when the streets were safe and a single, unarmed Bobby could disperse an angry crowd with a few well-chosen, authoritative words. Of course there was poverty, deprivation, crime and disease, but it was, we tend to think, in general a peaceful era, with Britain moving majestically towards the high-water mark of Empire.

The problem with this traditional idea of life during Victoria's reign is that it is almost wholly false and misleading. In fact, from Victoria's accession to the throne in 1837 until her death in 1901, Britain was a nation in turmoil. This can be most clearly seen when we look at what was happening on the streets throughout the Victorian period. From gun crime and terrorist attacks, to mugging, riots, sabotage, industrial unrest and the murder of police officers; the Victorians had many of today's problems to contend with and often to a far greater extent than we have in the twenty-first century. Little of this is reflected in the literature of the time and may consequently come as a something of a shock to many readers. A simple example will illustrate the point.

In 1842, England was gripped by a General Strike, which was marked by widespread and ferocious rioting, an organized campaign of sabotage and the imposition of something approaching martial law in the North of England. Troops opened fire on crowds of strikers, causing deaths in Preston, Blackburn and Halifax. It is interesting to see how this revolutionary period is dealt with in the novels written at about the time that these momentous events were taking place. It is from such novels, rather than from studying the history of those years, that many of us form our ideas about Victorian Britain.

One of Dickens' most popular books, *David Copperfield*, contains a brief reference to the strikes and disturbances in northern England. Headmaster Dr Strong asks his wife's cousin, Jack Maldon, if there is any news in the papers, to which Maldon replies: 'Nothing at all, sir. There's an account about the people being hungry and discontented down in the North, but they are always being hungry and discontented somewhere.' And that, as far as the General Strike and military repression of the workers in Yorkshire, is it! There is also mention of the matter in *Jane Eyre*, but in an even more cursory fashion. A character remarks: 'I have been *so* gay during my stay at S_____. Last night, or rather this morning, I was dancing till two o'clock. The _____ th regiment are stationed there since the riots.'

Even books which purport to show the reality of the Industrial Revolution in northern England, Dickens' *Hard Times*, for example, or Gaskell's *North and South*, present a bowdlerized perspective of society, in which the most prominent features of life in nineteenth-century Manchester are romances among the well-to-do.

This rosy view of life in nineteenth-century Britain, so commonly held, can cause problems when trying to examine and understand modern society. It often seems that we live in alarming and uncertain times; with violent crime, terrorism or civil disorder never far around the corner. This jaded view of the world may be blamed partly upon the mass media, who joyfully seize upon anything which might be exploited for the purposes of creating a good story.

Now, it is of course the custom of journalists and commentators to treat *any* event, even the slightest bit out of the ordinary, as being utterly remarkable and wholly unprecedented. Whether it is high winds, hot weather, floods, terrorism or rioting; the television and newspapers are always ready to assure us that such things have never before been known in Britain or are, at the very least, the worst on record. When this sort of thing is said of modern crimes and disturbances, it gives us the impression that we live in a uniquely dangerous era and that the prevalence of gun crime, threat of terrorism or scale of rioting has never been greater. We saw this with the rioting which gripped some English cities in the summer of 2011 and it is often asserted of crimes ranging from mugging to the possession and use of firearms. The murder of a police officer is a fairly unusual crime today and one that invariably catches the headlines; exploring the statistics of such crime helps draw useful comparisons with the Victorian era.

When PC Keith Blakelock was hacked to death by a frenzied mob in the 1985 Broadwater Farm riot, the murder was widely treated as a shocking and hitherto unknown type of crime in Britain. It was said that this was the first time a British police officer had been killed under such circumstances. In fact, for much of the nineteenth-century, the beating, stabbing and shooting to death of police officers by enraged crowds was a regular, and largely unremarkable, occurrence in this country. In the decade following the coronation of Queen Victoria in 1838, no fewer than sixteen police officers were murdered by rioting mobs. Some of the disturbances preceding these murders were political, but most were not. Attacking the police was simply a popular entertainment for a large number of working-class men and an opportunity to kick, punch and even stab or shoot a constable was relished.

These days, the killing of police officers in the execution of their duty is vanishingly rare. In the ten years preceding 2013, the last complete year for which records are available at the time of writing, not a single police officer was murdered in London. By contrast, in the course of a typical decade during the reign of Queen Victoria, 1860 to 1870, nine policemen were shot dead, beaten or stabbed to death in the Metropolitan area. Such attacks were not limited to the inner cities; the murder of police officers being just as common in rural areas as it was in towns. Between 1875 and 1895, for example, seventeen police officers were shot dead in Britain. Two were killed in London and one in Manchester; the rest died in more rural parts of the country such as Wiltshire, Cumberland, Berkshire, Staffordshire, Essex and Cleveland. This is roughly twice as many police officers as have been shot dead in Britain in the last twenty years.

Another modern trend, which a lot of us regard as a response to the hazardous times in which we live, is the visible arming of police officers. We have a mistaken idea that our police have traditionally been unarmed and that the sight of a police officer carrying a gun is a fairly recent development. This is quite untrue. The widespread carrying and use of firearms by criminals in the 1870s and 1880s, combined with a terrorist campaign being waged at that time in England and Scotland, led to the routine arming of police in many districts. From 1884 onwards, officers on duty at night in London suburbs were issued with revolvers upon request. In 1885 the Essex Constabulary also began to arm their officers at night and other forces followed suit. Even forces in completely rural areas, such as Cumberland and Westmorland were issuing revolvers to their officers regularly from the mid-1880s onwards. It is a sobering thought that, despite the common belief that the sight of police officers carrying pistols at their hips is symptomatic of the dangers of the modern world, as the nineteenth-century drew to a close, many police officers carried firearms every time they went on duty after dark.

Returning to the question of rioting and disorder, it was suggested during the riots of August 2011 that it might be necessary to deploy troops to restore order. This was widely regarded both by certain sections of the media and also some politicians as a sign that society was cracking under the strain of the widespread civil disorder and that order was altogether breaking down. It has perhaps been forgotten that during the whole of the Victorian period, and well into the twentieth century, soldiers were regularly called upon to combat civil disorder. It was by no means uncommon in nineteenth-century Britain for troops to open fire on crowds of protestors or to use force to disperse rioters. At times, whole districts were virtually under the control of the military. Most of these incidents are quite unknown today. The original 'Bloody Sunday' took place not in Northern Ireland but in Trafalgar Square, the heart of London, when, in 1887, a political meeting was declared illegal and a magistrate brought under military escort to read the Riot Act. The Grenadier Guards paraded with fixed bayonets and the cavalry were held in reserve in nearby streets. During the course of the fighting which followed, three demonstrators were killed. The suggestion was made that these deaths were caused by heavy handed behavior on the part of the police.

The readiness of the authorities to call out the military at the first sign of trouble is also evident in the events which gripped the seaside town of Worthing, on the south coast, in 1884 when the Salvation Army began holding meetings in the town, a move which was opposed by local publicans. There was some scuffling and a few fistfights, followed by shooting; the result was that a troop of cavalry was despatched to the town from nearby Brighton to quell the disorder.

The situation with terrorism in nineteenth-century Britain was also not much better than it is in modern times. The worst loss of life in a terrorist bombing in London, prior to the 7/7 attacks of 2005, took place in 1867, when fifteen men, women and children were killed by the detonation of a quarter of a ton of explosives in central London. The first tube bombings took place not during the IRA campaigns of the 1970s and 1980s, but in October 1883, with the first death in a bomb explosion on the underground coming in 1897.

In fact, many of the less attractive aspects of modern life, those that we assume are strange and atypical aberrations of the modern world, are really traditional British practices, dating back to the nineteenth-century. These include rioting, the killing of police officers by angry mobs, terrorist attacks, gun crime and mugging. All have been with us for centuries, but to understand how these things became an enduring feature of the Victorian era, we need to look at what was happening in the years before Victoria came to the throne.

Chapter 1

His Majesty, King Mob:
Tumult and Disorder in the Years
Leading up to the Victorian Period

Europe in the late-eighteenth-century, and a capital city is in flames. For almost a week, a vast crowd of discontented citizenry, over 50,000 strong, has raged through the streets; looting, burning and destroying property wholesale. The main prison has been stormed and the inmates freed; the central bank besieged and the home of the chief judge ransacked before being razed to the ground. In desperation, the king orders the military into action; giving them permission to take any steps necessary to restore order. Hundreds die as the troops repeatedly fire volleys of shots at those who seem intent on destroying the city and overthrowing the established order.

Surely, this can only be a description of Paris during the revolution which overthrew the monarchy in 1789? In fact, it is London in 1780; in the grip of the disturbances which became known as the Gordon Riots. It has been estimated that more damage was caused to London during that week than was inflicted on Paris in the week following the storming of the Bastille.

Those unfamiliar with the Gordon Riots might be a little taken aback to learn of the ostensible reason for such furious anger and wanton destruction, which almost led to the king abandoning his capital city. These bloody disturbances were precipitated by the 1778 Catholic Relief Act, which removed the legal prohibitions on Catholic priests holding services and also allowed for the inheritance of land by Catholics. None of these provisions could possibly have made the slightest bit of difference to the thousands of people who surged through London's streets, wreaking havoc wherever they could.

During the rioting in 2011, it was widely observed by some members of the press that many of the rioters were seemingly motivated less by the death of a young man in north London, the supposed trigger for the disorder, and more by the desire to loot and burn. Nor was it only right-wing newspapers such as *The Daily Mail* who drew such conclusions. As part of an analysis of the riots funded by the Joseph Rowntree Foundation and conducted jointly by *The Guardian* newspaper and the London School of Economics, young rioters themselves were interviewed at length. As the executive summary at the beginning of the report, entitled *Reading the Riots*, said;

> *Many rioters conceded their involvement in looting was simply down to opportunism, saying that a perceived suspension of normal rules presented them with an opportunity to acquire goods and luxury items they could not ordinarily afford. They often described the riots as a chance to obtain "free stuff".*

This seemed, somehow, to make the whole thing more shocking. These young people were not really protesting about a specific, supposed injustice; they were rebelling against society in general, seizing what they could carry away and burning what they could not. Far from being a shocking, modern phenomenon, caused, according to some, by lax parenting and poor discipline in schools, behaviour of this sort is really a recurring theme over many centuries in Britain.

There is a clue to the causes of the Gordon Riots of 1780, as well as the riots in Victorian Britain and possibly even the mob murders of police officers in the nineteenth-century, which may be found in a graffito scrawled on the wall of Newgate Prison after it had been sacked and the inmates released during the Gordon Riots. Newgate was the most famous prison in the land and a symbol of state power

to the inhabitants of London at that time. Freeing the prisoners and
then torching the building must have appeared a perfectly logical step
to take during a time of such licence. Written on the wall of the prison,
in letters 2 feet high, was the proclamation that the prisoners had all
been released; 'By order of His Majesty, King Mob'. This requires a
little explanation.

During the late seventeenth and early eighteenth-centuries, it was
the habit among the upper classes to refer to gatherings of ordinary
people as the *mobile vulgaris*; a Latin phrase meaning the fickle crowd.
This became abbreviated to the 'mobile'; an expression used for any
crowd of common people. In a mocking contrast to the word, 'nobility',
the working classes and peasants were sometimes referred to as the
'mobility'. In time, this was shortened to just 'mob'; a word which soon
became a contemptuous description applied to any disorderly crowd.
As sometimes happens, those to whom a faintly insulting epithet was
applied adopted it themselves and began to use it proudly. Describing
one's self as belonging to the mob became almost a badge of honour.

Contemporary writers who described the Gordon Riots expressed
surprise at the scale of destruction which was carried out without any
apparent benefit to the tens of thousands of people who had taken to the
streets. True, there was some looting, but there was a good deal more
burning and vandalism. These were men and women who seemingly
wished to strike at those above them on the social scale, rather than
seeking any personal advantage from what they could steal. Hardly
anybody had the right to vote at that time and the overwhelming
majority of ordinary people had absolutely no power nor the least
influence on how the country or its institutions were run. During a
riot, such people *did* have some power; if only for a few hours. Not
unnaturally, they tended to make the most of these brief periods of
ascendancy.

Throughout the eighteenth and nineteenth centuries, the streets
were often dangerous places for those with money or a superior

position. Whatever the nominal reasons for unrest, and these varied from Catholic Emancipation to tariff reform and the relief of the unemployed, the targets of the crowds' anger were often institutions which, on the face of it, had little to do with the crowds' grievances. During the Gordon Riots, the Bank of England, Lord Chief Justice's house and the prisons were all stormed by the mob. None of these locations could really be thought of as bastions of Catholicism; fierce disapproval of which was the supposed reason for the rioting. A century later, in 1886, during what became known as Black Monday, the demonstrators claimed to be worried about tariff reform and the provision being made for the unemployed. Their concern expressed itself in a rampage through the West End of London; smashing the windows of grand hotels and clubs, looting shops and assaulting and robbing anybody who appeared to be well-to-do. Liveried coachmen working for noble families were also attacked and stripped of their uniforms. What was really happening was discontented people at the bottom of the social system taking a welcome opportunity to lash out, by smashing windows and attacking those above them on the social scale. An instance from a few centuries earlier, also shows this phenomenon in action.

In the spring of 1517, there was uneasiness and anger among young, working-class Londoners about the number of foreigners moving into the city and, it was popularly supposed, taking the jobs of native-born Englishmen. Apprentices in particular were enraged about the flood of cheap labour from abroad. Rumours began to circulate that 1 May 1517 would be a day of reckoning for these impudent foreigners. May Day was traditionally a time of license and rowdiness for the young in Tudor England and the authorities were sufficiently alarmed to impose a curfew in London on the eve of May Day; ordering everybody to remain in their homes from 9.00 pm on the evening of 30 April. The apprentices and other young men ignored the curfew and began to congregate in large groups. Although their grievance, theoretically, concerned foreigners, this was soon forgotten as they began drinking, stealing and breaking windows. It soon became apparent that the question of imported labour was only the pretext for riot and disorder; the real purpose was for young people to run wild in the streets and do as they wished for a few days. After all, trouble caused by boisterous apprentices during the sixteenth century was anything but uncommon.

Troops were summoned to London from the provinces and by 5 May, over 5,000 soldiers were stationed in and around the city. Thirteen ringleaders of the riot were subsequently hanged. The event went down in history as, 'The Evil May Day'. It was really just one other incident of young men becoming high spirited and their behaviour getting out of hand. As Roy Porter points out in *A Social History of London*, apprentices did, from time to time, make a nuisance of themselves in Tudor London. In 1576 householders were reminded that their apprentices must not 'misuse, molest or evil treat' respectable people in the streets. Two years later, the Shrove Tuesday holiday had to be suspended because of the 'great disorders, uncomely and dangerous behaviors' of the young apprentices. There was even the Tudor equivalent of football hooligans, when, in 1590, three journeymen were imprisoned for, 'outrageously and riotously behaving themselves at football play in Cheapside'. Some of these events were merely hooliganism, others developed into riots, but the same underlying atmosphere existed as in later centuries. The underprivileged in society were always on the lookout, on various pretexts, to break free and strike out at the social system.

Similar, in many ways, to both the Gordon Riots and incidents like the Evil May Day were the murders of police officers by mobs, which became something of a feature of Victorian Britain. The disturbances which led to these murders had, ostensibly, many different causes but were all essentially motivated by the desire of the lowly and powerless to assert themselves. The uniformed police officer in early Victorian Britain was often the most visible, accessible and vulnerable symbol of authority which the average person would regularly encounter. A blow against the police was a challenge to the established order. For men lacking even a vote, attacking police officers was a way of registering disapproval and making their dissatisfaction known.

The main difference between crime and unrest in the sixty-three years of Victoria's reign and any other period of British history is that this was the time when modern police forces were being set up across Britain. Prior to this, rioting, violent crime and disorder were usually dealt with by the army but this became increasingly impractical after the Industrial Revolution. It is one thing to use a squadron of cavalry to drive off a crowd of mutinous peasants in open country, but the same tactics are unlikely to work well in a city. As the population of Britain began the inexorable movement from the countryside to the towns and cities, so disorder and crime needed to be dealt with differently.

Even as early as the Tudor period, using the army to handle civil unrest in towns was seen to be a tricky and uncertain business. On the Evil May Day of 1517, for example, the Lieutenant of the Tower of London was ordered to prepare his artillery for use against the mobs roaming through the streets of London. Several cannons were fired, which injured nobody but caused considerable damage to a number of houses. The discharge of the cannons failed to calm those taking part in the disorder.

One of the chief disadvantages of using soldiers to quell rioting and disorder is that they are seldom equipped to take half measures. It is in the nature of armies that their members are trained to kill the enemy as expeditiously as possible. On a foreign battlefield, such tactics are praiseworthy but when the enemy is your own discontented citizenry, their wholesale slaughter is apt to cause concern; even among the most diehard reactionaries. As guardians of public order, the armed forces are far from ideal.

The deadly nature of military force when used for crowd control was tacitly recognized when framing the 1714 Riot Act, which became law the following year, was frequently used during the nineteenth-century and remained in force in parts of the UK until 1973. Under this act, a magistrate, mayor or other public figure could order people to disperse to their homes if there seemed to be the chance of a riot developing. It is important to note that the people present did not need to be actually *doing* anything; their very presence was enough. If twelve or more people were, 'unlawfully, riotously and tumultuously assembled together', then a declaration in accordance with the Riot Act could be read out. Those who remained an hour later could, in theory, be killed with impunity by troops! The Riot Act was regularly read during demonstrations, strikes and gatherings throughout the nineteenth-century and was last used in Liverpool and Glasgow in 1919.

The wording of the proclamation that had to be read was laid down by law and was to be strictly adhered to; otherwise, suppressing the riot might be unlawful. Here are the words used:

Our Sovereign Lord the King chargeth and commandeth all persons, being assembled, immediately to disperse themselves, and peaceably depart to their habitations, or to their lawful business, upon the pains contained in the Act made in the first year of King George the First for preventing tumults and riotous assemblies. God save the King.

This form of words had to be followed exactly. On one occasion the courts ruled that those charged with riot could not be convicted, because the words 'God save the King' had been left out when the Riot Act was read.

Two things need to be remembered. First, the people assembled did not need to be actually doing anything, other than looking as though they might create a disturbance, for the Riot Act to be read. The second point to consider is that once the Riot Act had been read and an hour had passed, the army could take absolutely any action, including opening fire at the crowd, without fear of any legal consequences. Anybody assisting in dispersing a group of people to whom the Riot

Act had been read, was specifically indemnified by the Act against being charged later as a result of any injuries or deaths which they might cause.

In effect, the Riot Act gave the authorities and the army *carte blanche* to shoot anybody in order to get a mob to disperse. As the Victorian age progressed, this became increasingly unacceptable and rather than calling on the military, efficient police forces were established, part of whose job was to maintain public order. Those in charge of Victorian Britain wished to see civilized behaviour on the streets; not the sort of scenes that one might expect in Hogarth's *Gin Lane*. A reluctance to use the armed forces to keep order in cities was part and parcel of this desire to see society conform to the middle-class view of respectable conduct. It is hard to maintain the pretence of a peaceful and prosperous city when the sound of gunfire can be heard outside the drawing room window or hussars can be seen riding down protestors and attacking them with sabres.

Although the need for a change in the way that public order was kept was apparent to many people, there was enormous opposition to the setting up of proper, permanent and paid police forces in Britain. The very idea of 'police' was viewed with grave suspicion, particularly from the middle classes. They looked at France and saw police being used as an instrument of state repression; spying on ordinary citizens on behalf of the government and seeking out dissent. The old and tried system of watchmen and parish constables might be inefficient and widely mocked and derided, but it had worked well enough for many years.

Deterring crime and tackling disorder in Georgian Britain had been achieved in two ways. Crime had been dealt with by imposing increasingly ferocious penalties, which prescribed the death penalty for over 200 offences ranging from piracy and murder to scratching graffiti on Westminster Bridge. The so-called 'Bloody Code' did not prevent crime, because the chances of actually being caught were so low. It is the likelihood of detection which discourages criminals; not savage sentences which they will almost certainly evade. From the end of the eighteenth-century, there were those, such as the MPs Sir William Meredith and Sir Samuel Romilly, who argued that hangings were merely retributive and did nothing to check crime. In 1819, the House of Commons appointed the Committee of Inquiry in the Criminal Laws, which came to much the same conclusion. This led, a decade later, to the establishment of Britain's first modern police force. From then on, the focus of penal policy moved from punishing harshly those few criminals who were actually caught, towards ensuring that more of those breaking the law were apprehended in the first place.

The old system for dealing with crime consisted of local areas and parishes, appointing a constable. If it became necessary to track down criminals, then a hue and cry could be raised in which any citizen might be expected to join. Temporary constables could also be sworn in to deal with specific emergencies. As the Industrial Revolution gathered pace, however, and the flow of people from the countryside to the cities became a flood, it was plain that a new system was needed for preventing crime and disorder. The only remedy seemed to be regular police forces following the continental pattern. This would entail a permanent force of professional officers; controlled by a central authority.

The growing middle classes in Britain opposed the idea of properly organized police forces not only for the fear that an effective police force might be used as the instrument of tyranny, but also for the more pragmatic reason of not wishing cities and counties to organize police forces which would be an expensive business and bound to drive up the rates paid by householders and shopkeepers. The existing system might often be ineffective, but it was cheap. If things did get out of hand, then calling out the military cost nothing at all.

The increasing lawlessness was becoming a scandal as Britain entered the nineteenth-century. In 1819, the disadvantages of using the armed forces to handle demonstrations and protests became apparent when cavalry charged a peaceful meeting held at St Peter's Field in Manchester. Hundreds of men and women were injured and about a dozen killed in the event which was later known as the Peterloo Massacre, in ironic reference to the Battle of Waterloo.

On the crime prevention front, the mass hangings of thieves and other petty criminals at Tyburn, among other places, which were such a popular feature of the late eighteenth-century, did not exactly accord with the new, civilized city life that the middle and upper classes were hoping to see. Reluctantly, it was realized that the only way to avoid massacres by the army and large scale public executions was to establish a police force and see if this tended to make for a more stable and orderly society. Where better to begin such an experiment than in the capital itself? So it was that in the autumn of 1829, almost ten years before Victoria came to the throne, the Metropolitan Police Force was established by Home Secretary Robert Peel.

The police were still regarded with a great deal of mistrust by respectable people, as well as outright hostility by the working classes. This mistrust and hostility combined to make life precarious for those first British police officers. This is no mere figure of speech; their lives were, quite literally, precarious, because there were many people in London who wished to murder them. These ranged from political agitators, to drunks wandering the streets after the closure of the local alehouse.

Before we look at the hazards faced by those first police officers though, we might consider what the actual purpose of the police is in this country. We are so used to having a uniformed and highly visible police force, that we seldom give much thought to their actual *raison d'etre*; we simply take them for granted. The role which we mostly associate with the police is, of course, the prevention and detection of crime. When they were founded in 1829 though, dealing with crime was only one facet of their work. The other was keeping the peace;

which is to say ensuring that the streets are safe and that there are no public disturbances or riots. Although this aspect of their work is less important than it was a couple of centuries ago, the police remain the ultimate guardians of the Queen's peace.

From the beginning of the first modern, British police force in 1829, the strategy of the British police with regard to public order has always been an ounce of prevention, rather than a pound of cure. In other words, they have moved to stop disorderly conduct before it actually develops into something worse. This strategy brought them into conflict, from the very first years of their existence, with large parts of the population; not only criminals but also many ordinary, working-class men and women who objected to what they saw as infringements on their traditional way of life. The resultant friction resulted in a number of deaths, such as those caused when police officers were beaten to death by the residents of slum districts, who regarded the patrolling police as hostile intruders into their own territory. It took several decades before the principle was firmly established that the police, rather than being the enemies of freedom, were actually its strongest and most devoted guardians.

Chapter 2

Killed in the Line of Duty: The Murder of Police Officers in the Early Years of Victoria's Reign

In the Introduction, PC Keith Blakelock's murder in 1985 was cited as an example of the sort of event which is often portrayed as being uniquely horrible and quite unprecedented. This particular violent death is sometimes thought of as marking a watershed in relations between the police and certain sections of society. Really, this is quite absurd; the murder of police officers in this way having begun almost as soon as police forces in the modern sense were established in this country. The deaths of police officers during disturbances on the streets of nineteenth-century Britain were a regular occurrence. In stark contrast to the banner headlines and widespread coverage, which greeted the murder of PC Blakelock in 1985 and also those of WPCs Yvonne Fletcher in the previous year and Sharon Beshenivsky in 2005, similar deaths in the late 1830s and 1840s rated only a few column inches in *The Times*.

On the night of Sunday, 29 September 1839, two years after Victoria became Queen, a police officer in London was killed by a 500-strong mob. On 1 October, *The Times* reported the incident under the brief headline; 'MURDER OF A POLICEMAN AT DEPTFORD'. Only four column inches were devoted to the death of a police officer in this way; a total of 350 words or so. It simply wasn't newsworthy. Among items which demanded greater coverage in that day's edition were the municipal reform of the Corporation of London and a shipwreck off the Maldives! The death of a police officer at the hands of a crowd was not so unusual as to merit more extensive reporting.

One of the first men to join the newly formed Metropolitan Police in 1829 was also one of the first police officers to die at the hands of a disorderly mob. There are many similarities between the murders of Keith Blakelock and Police Constable Robert Culley and it is interesting to examine the earlier case in some detail, for the light it sheds on the way that the police were viewed by many in nineteenth-century Britain and how attitudes have radically changed since then.

When London's Metropolitan Police Force was established in September 1829, one of the first to sign up was 23 year-old Robert Culley. Many of the new officers did not last long, the standards for the new force being considerably higher than had been the case with the old Parish Constables. Police Constable No 95 stuck at it and by the spring of 1833, was one of the longest-serving officers in London. By that time, Culley had been married for two years and was living in central London, near Leicester Square.

Despite the extension of the franchise brought about by the *1832 Reform Act*, many working-class men were still dissatisfied with the situation around voting. After all, over 90 per cent of adults were still unable to vote. Some believed that every man should be entitled to vote in elections; a handful of extremists even thought that women too should be given the vote. An organization called the National Union of the Working Classes arranged to hold a meeting at Coldbath Fields in the London district of Clerkenwell. To the government, this smacked of sedition and Home Secretary Lord Melbourne issued a proclamation forbidding any such assembly to be held. The public notice from the Home Office read as follows;

Posters have been put up and distributed in various parts of London, advertising that a meeting will be held in Coldbath Fields on Monday 13 May, as a means of campaigning for the rights of the people. A

*public meeting held for such a purpose is dangerous to the public peace,
and illegal. All classes of His Majesty's subjects are hereby warned
not to attend such a meeting, nor to take any part in it. Notice is
hereby given that the police have strict orders to maintain and secure
the public peace, and to arrest anybody offending against this order, so
that they may be dealt with according to the law.*

The legality of this prohibition was open to question. Why should a
public meeting to campaign for the rights of the people be thought
automatically to be dangerous to the public peace? What was illegal
about such a meeting? Nevertheless, it was the duty of the police to
obey the Home Secretary and posters were put up, warning people
not to attend the demonstration. Then, as now, there were those who
objected to what they saw as unwarranted interference on the part of
the executive in the execution of their liberties and the meeting went
ahead anyway.

Since a good deal of the violence and civil disorder in eighteenth-
and nineteenth-century Britain was caused by the rage of the working
class at their powerlessness, it is worth considering what happened to
precipitate the violence at Coldbath Fields. The Great Reform Bill
of 1832 had extended the franchise from around 400,000 to 650,000;
perhaps one in five of the adult male population. This still meant that
at least 90 per cent of the population had no say in the running of the
country. As Edward Vallance remarks in *A Radical History of Britain*,
this meant that these male voters after 1832 actually comprised a
smaller proportion of the population than those who had had the vote
in 1640, before the English Civil War! Small wonder that there was
discontent among both the urban working class and the rural peasantry
at such a state of affairs. Even planning a peaceful protest at the system
which denied them the franchise, was met with the threat of force;
the government announced that even campaigning for the extension
of the franchise to the working classes was a danger to the public

peace! Unsurprisingly, with even peaceful political activity forbidden, some people reacted by fighting against what they saw as tyranny and the most visible symbol of their repression: the hated police. This happened not only in a political sense, but was also a common feeling among those leaving the public houses. The police strategy during the demonstration in Coldbath Fields consisted of what is referred to today as 'kettling'; which means confining protestors in a small area until they have 'cooled down'. On 13 May 1833, this tactic backfired in the most spectacular way imaginable. The aim of the police was to prevent a riot; instead, they precipitated one.

The meeting in Coldbath Fields began as scheduled, with speakers addressing the crowd from open wagons, which were being used as platforms. The police managed to disperse some of the audience peacefully, but it became clear that some of those present had come prepared for a confrontation. Banners were carried on poles tipped with sharp points. These were, in effect, pikes or spears and the police were keen to remove such potentially deadly weapons from the scene. As some of the men attending the meeting were shepherded away from Coldbath Fields by the police, another column of police formed ranks in Calthorpe Street and prevented the protestors from leaving the area. It was at this point that things went horribly wrong.

Calthorpe Street has changed little since that day in 1833; tall, dark terraces of late-Georgian town houses with wrought iron balconies still line the narrow street. There are a number of eyewitness accounts from the people living in those houses, who watched the tragedy unfold from their balconies. Some of the streets in the area are still cobbled, rather than covered with tarmac, and it is very easy when walking around the district to visualize precisely how the tragedy unfolded.

The men being pushed up Calthorpe Street from one end, and hemmed in from the other, were in no mood to be confined in that way. They began to grow restless and attempted to fight their way free of the police cordon. It was at this point that the police officers drew their batons. The street became a seething mass of angry men; punching, kicking and lashing out at each other with anything that came to hand. A hail of stones and half bricks rained down on the police lines. Sergeant John Brooks, who had spent twenty-five years in the army before joining the police, decided to remove some of the poles that were being waved about by the protestors. He grabbed at an American flag, which was being carried by a man called George Fursey who at once pulled out a dagger and stabbed Sergeant Brooks in the chest. By great good fortune, the blade struck a rib; otherwise, it would, according to the surgeon who later treated him, have slid straight into the man's heart. Brooks fell back with a cry, upon which PC Henry Redwood tried to snatch the flag. Fursey stabbed him as well, through the forearm. Redwood responded by beating Fursey over the head with his baton and handing him to two other officers to be arrested.

While Sergeant Brooks and PC Redwood were being stabbed, another group of police officers had become separated from their comrades and were surrounded by a screaming mob. One of them, Robert Culley, cried out that he had been hurt. He managed to break free and stagger into a nearby public house, the Calthorpe Arms. PC No 95 Culley collapsed once inside the pub and died with his head being cradled in the lap of a barmaid.

The contrast between the reaction to Keith Blakelock's death in a riot in 1985 and the public attitude to that of Robert Culley in similar circumstances a century and a half earlier is truly astonishing and sheds light on the way that the police were widely viewed in Britain at that time. It will be remembered that there was widespread outrage and disgust at the stabbing to death of a police officer during the disturbances at Tottenham in 1985. Condemnation of the murder was all but universal, among all classes and types of people. How very different was the response to PC Culley's death in 1833.

Events moved at breakneck speed after Robert Culley was stabbed to death on the Monday. The inquest opened less than forty-eight hours later, being convened on Wednesday, 15 May. It was held in an upstairs room of the Calthorpe Arms; the very building in which the police officer had died. This building, too, is still standing and is largely unaltered since those days. From the beginning, it was obvious that the jury were ill-disposed towards the police. The members of this jury were far from being hot-headed young radicals; they were shopkeepers and householders from the surrounding district. After several sharp exchanges with the coroner, they eventually brought in a verdict not of murder or even manslaughter, but of justifiable homicide on the part of the person who killed PC Culley. They explained this extraordinary verdict by citing, 'the conduct of the police', was, they claimed, 'ferocious, brutal and unprovoked by the people'.

On Saturday, 17 May, four days after his death, Robert Culley's funeral was held at St Anne's church in Soho, near to his home. His heavily pregnant wife attended the service. Some 300 people were gathered outside the church, to greet the funeral cortege with catcalls and jeers. Newspapers expressed shock at this behaviour, but there was no doubt that many ordinary people thought that PC Culley had richly deserved to be stabbed to death by a member of the infuriated mob.

The individual members of the jury had already been accompanied home at the end of the inquest by torchlit processions. These parades were cheered by passers-by, who were keen to show their approval of the jurors for delivering their verdict of justifiable homicide. The following month, a group of radicals called the Milton Street Committee arranged a trip up the Thames for the jurors and their families to Twickenham. Although it was a rainy day, crowds lined the banks of the River Thames to cheer the boat as it passed. Costemongers, city clerks and shopkeepers were all determined to turn out, in spite of the heavy downpour, to voice their support for the blow that the seventeen men had struck for liberty. Nothing could more clearly demonstrate the feelings of ordinary people towards the new police force

Today, we find such an attitude on the part of the public all but incomprehensible. The idea of a funeral being disrupted in this way would be unthinkable. A lot of people believed that this had been a blow for liberty and that striking at the police in this way was perfectly acceptable.

The coroner's jury was not the only one that year to give what seemed to the authorities a perverse verdict. George Fursey was arraigned at the Old Bailey in July, charged with the malicious wounding of Sergeant Brookes and PC Redwood. The evidence was plain and there could be little doubt that the man in the dock had lashed out with a dagger at two police officers. Nevertheless, he was acquitted and carried home from the court on the shoulders of well-wishers.

The antagonism felt by working people towards authority, of whom the police were the visible and public representatives, became endemic from the very day of the young Victoria's coronation. One constable was killed by a crowd celebrating the coronation itself. A typical example of the way in which the murderous rage of the mob could flare up at any moment is provided by the murder of another police officer, which took place a year after the coronation. The murder of constable William Aldridge on the evening of Sunday, 29 September 1839 is typical of the hazards faced by the police at this time. There had been a lot of rowdy behaviour in the Navy Arms pub in Deptford, a district in south London, that evening and the landlady had asked the police to intervene. Two of those who had been swearing and making a nuisance of themselves were brothers William and John Pine. William was twenty and his brother twenty-one. These two young men began larking around in the street after leaving the pub and PC George Stevens told them to calm down or he would have to arrest them. One thing led to another and John Pine punched the officer, who responded by drawing his truncheon and rapping the drunk man over the head with it before arresting him. In no time at all, a crowd gathered which was determined to rescue Pine from the police. At this point, constable William Aldridge appeared on the scene to help take charge of John Pine. Over 200 people surrounded the two police officers with, more arriving every minute as word spread around the neighbourhood that a 'rescue' was in progress. It was an ugly situation, but the two men were determined not to let their prisoner walk free.

As the constables continued to drag John Pine off, the crowd pelted them with rocks and stones. By this time, it was estimated by both the police and local witnesses who later spoke to newspaper reporters that between 500 and 600 people were attacking constables Aldridge and Stevens. Two more police officers arrived to help, but the four of them were forced to flee from the mob. PC No 204 William Aldridge went down, struck on the head by a large rock and he died at 4.30 the following morning.

Three weeks later the Pine brothers, who were well known to the police, found themselves on trial at the Old Bailey for murder. In the dock with them were two other men who had taken leading roles in the riot; William Calvert and John Burke. The evidence was clear enough and the men were fortunate not to hang for their actions. As it was, they were convicted of the lesser charge of manslaughter. John Pine was sentenced to transportation for life to Australia, along with Calvert, who was transported for fifteen years. The other two men received two years imprisonment each.

The deaths of Robert Culley and William Aldridge are, at least on the face of it, very different. One can be seen as a political murder, almost an act of rebellion against the establishment; the other a sordid row after closing time at the local pub. They had features in common, though, and are more similar than might at first appear.

When it was founded, London's new police force had two aims. One was the prevention of crime; to which few, other than the criminals themselves, could object. The other was the maintenance of public order, and it was this which made them unpopular in many quarters from the very beginning. The reason was that various classes and sections of the public had very different notions about what constituted good public order. For some, it simply meant being able to walk the streets after dark without fear of being robbed or assaulted. For the government of the day, however, maintaining public order could mean the prevention of any gatherings of citizens who wished to change the terms of the franchise. It was for the working class that this new idea of keeping order on the streets presented the most difficulties.

Most working-class people at this time lived in poky, cramped and unattractive conditions. It was not uncommon for twenty, thirty or even forty people to share one house. The Industrial Revolution meant that the majority of ordinary workers now lived in towns and cities, rather than rural areas; which in turn meant that spending time outdoors was virtually synonymous with being on the streets. It was on the streets and other public spaces that working-class men, women and children carried on their social lives and pursued their leisure activities. They chatted with friends, gambled, sang, played games, fought, drank, flirted, traded and conducted the greater part of their lives in public. It was this traditional lifestyle, a natural development of the village life which families had pursued until moving to the cities, that was threatened by the idea of an orderly urban environment. It was one thing to cavort in fields and meadows or even on a village green; behaving in the same way in a city was something else. Those who mattered in Victorian society did not wish to see half-naked urchins rolling in the gutters or men fighting in the street. It was not only the ruling classes who felt this way; the burgeoning middle class also did not wish to see beggars, costermongers, prostitutes or barefoot children thronging the pavements. Nor did they approve of public lovemaking or drunkenness. They wished for the city streets to be respectable and clean; with a strict separation between private and public activities. Ideally, they wanted everybody to stay in their homes, unless they were actually travelling through the streets for some purpose or from one place to another. The idea of people using the city streets as a living space was anathema to those tidy minded people who ruled Victorian Britain.

This was very much a development of the Industrial Revolution. The Georgian gentry had been more or less indifferent to such matters. It was the Victorian bourgeoise who were so readily shocked by the conduct of the 'lower orders'. The people to whom they looked to protect their sensibilities were the new police officers.

The police were charged with patrolling the streets and changing the way that the working classes comported themselves in public. In effect, police officers were expected to impose middle-class values and ways of behaving upon every person out in public. This caused friction between them and the people whom they chivvied about and whose way of life they wished so radically to modify.

The two murders that we have looked at so far in this chapter illustrate these points with great clarity. On the one hand, the police were expected to prevent dissent against the government and to break up meetings calling for greater political rights for working-class men. It was believed that police officers were enforcing the will of the government and behaving as though they were soldiers fighting an enemy. Opposition to the police was seen as standing up for an Englishman's liberties. This is why Robert Culley's death was classed by a jury of respectable shopkeepers as justifiable homicide

William Aldridge's death was provoked by the most trifling of causes. The Pine brothers had been wrestling in the street; something which fifty years earlier might not have raised eyebrows. Now though, the police felt it their duty to put a stop to such horseplay in public, and the consequence was a man's death. Many working men and women were defending their way of life and if the police wished to try and challenge them, then so much the worse for them! In both of the above cases, the police were identified with the ruling class and attacks on them were really aimed at the established order, no matter what trivial cause had precipitated the violence. One spark which set off many violent clashes between the police and those living in impoverished areas was the so-called 'freedom riot'. PC Aldridge's death was a result of a 'freedom riot', which were very common in eighteenth- and nineteenth-century Britain. If a police officer had arrested somebody in a working-class district, then the cry of 'Rescue!' would go up. Any men and women within earshot would surround the constable and his prisoner, in an attempt to intimidate the policeman into freeing the person he had detained. Sometimes, this end could be achieved without violence; just by creating an atmosphere of confusion and hustling the prisoner away while the attention of the police officer was distracted. Sometimes this worked, but at other times it did not. On occasions, the consequences could be tragic.

In the mid-nineteenth-century, the streets of London's East End were notorious for crime and disorderly behaviour. When, in the early hours of 22 September 1841, PC Carroll was walking his beat in the district of Shoreditch, he took exception to what was described by another officer as the 'riotous behaviour' of a man. Carroll duly arrested the man and tried to lead his prisoner to the police station. It was at that point that things began to go seriously wrong. Helped by another officer, Carroll took the man he had arrested past a pub called the Knave of Hearts which, despite the lateness of the hour, was still doing a roaring trade. As they passed by, a man called Thomas Smedley approached them and, grabbing both police officers by their collars, shouted that they would not take the man away. According to the officer who came to Carroll's aid, Police Constable H194 George Townsend, what Smedley actually said was: 'You bastards shall not take him. You shall let him go!' There was a brief argument before Smedley punched PC Carroll and knocked him down. The traditional cry of 'Rescue!' was raised by those now spilling out of the pub and a crowd soon gathered. The other constable, George Townsend, was also struck and he responded by lashing out at those near at hand with his truncheon. In the course of this melee, the prisoner escaped.

Annoyed with Thomas Smedley for his role in effecting the escape of their prisoner, the constables then attempted, unsuccessfuly, to arrest him instead. Alerted by the shouting, people ran from nearby houses and joined the mob already surrounding the two constables. The situation was extremely threatening and PC Carroll tried to use his truncheon to force a way through the crowd. According to PC Townsend, there were shouts of, 'Murder the bastards!' and, 'Don't let them take anybody!' Smedley managed to wrest Carroll's truncheon from the officer and struck him over the head with it. As soon as Carroll fell to the ground, the crowd began to kick him. He died a short while later.

As a result of more police appearing on the scene, Thomas Smedley was seized and taken to the police station in Bethnal Green. He was later charged with the murder of PC Carroll. The inquest on the officer returned a verdict of wilful murder against Smedley and he was committed for trial at the Old Bailey.

On Friday, 29 October 1841, Thomas Smedley appeared in the dock at the Old Bailey. It was widely assumed that the case against him was merely a formality and that he would soon be found guilty and hanged. The prosecution, though, was reluctant to pursue the murder charge. So many people had been involved in beating and kicking PC Carroll to death, that it was impossible to say what part the prisoner in the dock had played in the tragedy. That he had struck the constable over the head was not disputed and Smedley readily pleaded guilty to the lesser charge of aggravated assault. He was sentenced to two years imprisonment with hard labour.

It was not only people in the poorer, working-class districts who relished the opportunity to strike at the police. Elections were far more riotous in the nineteenth-century than is the case today. Fights between individual supporters of the political parties were common, as were general brawls in which everybody might join. The police, whose job it was to separate the warring factions, often came off worse. When things became heated at the election in Carlisle on 29 June 1841, for example, a constable attempted to restore order, with fatal consequences.

Before the secret ballot was introduced to this country in 1872, voters declared their vote publicly. This frequently led to heckling, jeers and shouts of disapproval. Tempers often became frayed as it became clear which way the election was moving. In the Carlisle election, the trouble began the day before the election itself, during speeches made by the candidates accepting their nominations. An angry crowd followed one of the candidates to the hotel where he was staying and began to pelt the building with sticks and stones. The police superintendent ordered his men to draw their truncheons and charge the men throwing stones. This led to a wild and confused fight, with many people knocked to the ground by the police. One officer, Thomas Jardine, was so enthusiastic in striking wildly with his truncheon, that he became separated from his fellows and ended up being surrounded by the crowd.

According to police evidence, a man called John Kirkpatrick was seen to take a club from his pocket and hit PC Jardine the head with it, knocking him to the ground. He tried to get up again, but another man, James Johnson, lashed out at him with a walking stick or staff. Jardine did not recover from the attack and died less than twelve hours later, from the injuries to his head.

At the trial of Kirkpatrick and Johnson for the murder of Thomas Jardine, which took place at the Carlisle Assizes on 5 August 1841, both men pleaded not guilty. Perhaps harking back to the killing of PC Culley less than ten years earlier, counsel for the men suggested that it was the fault of the police that the murder had taken place. He expressed the view that some rowdy behaviour was inevitable during an election and if the police had not intervened, then things would have calmed down. He went on:

If the police had not so placed themselves in opposition, as it were to the crowd, who on such occasions did and had a right to express their approbation or disapprobation of the conduct and principles of those who were candidates for the high office of making laws, to affect the lives, the liberties and rights of that very multitude, in all probability their excited feelings would have evaporated in throwing a few comparatively harmless missiles which might have rendered it necessary to wash a few spots of mud from the front of the hotel or to repair a few broken panes of glass, in all probability no blood would have been shed.

In other words, if the police had left the crowd to riot, nobody would have been hurt and only a bit of damage would have been caused.

The judge, Lord Denman, was not impressed by this line of defence and directed the jury to disregard it. James Johnson was entirely acquitted by the jury and John Kirkpatrick acquitted of murder, but convicted of the lesser charge of manslaughter. Little good it did him, because he was sentenced to be transported to Australia for fifteen years.

Yet another instance from 5 May 1851, helps illustrate the prevalence of violence towards the police. Constables Edward Newton and Henry James Chaplin were passing along Vauxhall Walk at about 1.00 am, when they heard a lot of noise coming from a nearby public house called The Pheasant. The public house was closing and a large crowd of rowdy and drunk young men had gathered outside the pub; singing, shouting and engaging in various kinds of horseplay. Newton and Chaplin approached the men and suggested that it might be time for them to think about getting to their homes and that, at the very least, they should make a little less noise as other people were trying to sleep.

So far, this is an unexceptional scenario, of the kind which is played out these days in every town in the United Kingdom on any Saturday night at about the same time. It was what happened next which showed how different things were at in those days. PC Newton crossed the road to speak to another large group of men who were making a disturbance. While he was talking to them, he left PC Chaplin standing by the pub. A number of those who had been asked to keep the noise down had equipped themselves with bricks and large stones and had fallen upon the policeman, beating him round the head with the obvious intention of killing him. PC Newton ran back, but the mob was now so threatening that he was forced to run for his life. He escaped amidst a hail of half bricks and large stones. When he had summoned help, Newton returned to the scene with a number of officers and found Henry Chaplin laying on the ground, almost dead. He died a few hours later.

The accounts given at the inquest into Chaplin's death of what injuries he had sustained make gruesome reading. According to Mr W. Rees, the surgeon who had conducted the autopsy, it was the damage to Chaplin's head which resulted in his death;

> *Upon the scalp were several large lacerated wounds, and on the skull, corresponding with these injuries, were as many fractures, several of them comminuted, and others of a simple kind extending entirely across the frontal and spheroid bones. The temporal muscles were crushed, the dura mater and brain lacerated, and the scalp and muscular textures were infiltrated with blood, and a large quantity of blood was found upon both hemispheres of the brain. There was scarcely a portion of the internal structure of the head which had escaped injury or partial destruction.*

In lay terms, the unfortunate police constable's head had been shattered to pieces by repeated and violent blows with bricks and stones.

A number of people were arrested and questioned about the death of PC Chaplin and eventually three of them were charged with murder. On 20 June 1851, Patrick Cane, a 40-year-old labourer, John Hickey,

23, and 19-year-old James M'Ellicott, a tailor, appeared in court. The evidence against two of the men, Cane and Hickey, was more or less incontrovertible. They were identified by the police and had been arrested with bloodstains on their hands and clothes. PC Thomas Streames, one of those fetched by Newton when he went for help, had entered a nearby house into which one of the suspects had been seen entering after the disturbance. He found Hickey hiding in the cellar and when brought out, the man had blood all over his hands.

That Cane and Hickey, at least, had been involved in the attack on the police officer seemed certain; that they had set out to kill him, was impossible to prove. The jury gave M'Ellicott the benefit of the doubt and acquitted him. Patrick Cane and James Hickey were acquitted of murder but found guilty of manslaughter. Mr Justice Coleridge, who presided over the trial, was determined to show what he felt about such an attack on the police. Both men were sentenced to be transported to Australia for fifteen years.

It is interesting to observe that although the Victorian penal system has now a reputation for being ferocious and uncompromising, quite a few of the verdicts and sentences are lighter than they would be today. These days, if a group of drunken hooligans beat a policeman to death by smashing his skull open and exposing his brain, it is very unlikely that they would be convicted only of manslaughter. Time and again, when looking at such cases, we see that wherever possible the courts did their utmost to be fair and give the men in the dock every possible benefit of the doubt.

Slowly, as the century progressed, the murder of police officers by mobs in this way became a less commonplace and unremarkable occurance. Assaults were still very common, but they were less likely to end in the death of the police officer. Well into the twentieth century it was still the custom to attack policemen, simply in order to discourage them from visiting certain streets and districts. But after the 1840s and 1850s, attacks of this kind were commonly made, only with fists and boots rather than knives. Old habits die hard, though, and cases of such murders, although rarer as the decades passed, continued throughout the whole of the nineteenth-century. Even as late as 1875, the death of a police officer at the hands of a crowd was not seen as remarkable.

On the night of Sunday, 7 March 1875, two police officers went to a public house in the Navigation Road area of Birmingham, to arrest a suspected burglar. The Navigation Road district was known to be a rough place, where police officers only patrolled in pairs. The man for whom the two policemen were looking was found in the Bull's Head pub and was arrested without any fuss. The aim was to remove him to the nearest police station. It was then that the trouble began.

Several hot-headed young men began to stir up the drinkers in the pub and urge them to rescue the arrested man. As the police moved away from the establishment, a crowd spilled out onto the pavement, incited by a 22-year-old man called Jeremiah Corkery. Corkery was heard to shout, 'Let's give it to the pigs!' Hard to believe that this was almost a century and a half ago!

People came out of nearby houses and joined the drinkers from the Bull's Head. In no time at all, a 'Freedom Riot' had developed; the aim of which was to release the man whom the police had detained. The noise attracted the attention of other police officers and they came running to the assistance of the two original officers, who were now surrounded by a large and extremely angry mob who were baying for their blood. It was less a question of managing to get their prisoner to the police station, than it was of saving their own lives. Bottles and bricks were thrown; punches and kicks were aimed at the police as the crowd closed in and then at least two people drew knives and began attacking the nearest police officers.

A sergeant was stabbed, although mercifully the wound was not a serious one, and then 30-year-old PC William Lines had his throat slashed. Lines had been in the police for eleven years and had been the victim of three serious assaults in the past. He slumped to the ground, mortally wounded. Although he lingered on for a week before dying, Lines was unable to identify the man who had stabbed him. This was left to other officers, who had managed to grab hold of Jeremiah Corkery; the man who had initiated the riot.

Once again, it is instructive to examine the newspaper coverage of this dreadful crime and compare it with the sort of thing we might expect these days after a disturbance in which a police officer with a young daughter had been stabbed to death by rioters. Here is how the *Manchester Guardian*, forerunner of today's *Guardian*, reported the case after the inquest on William Lines. In the edition for 29 March, there was a small piece consisting of just thirteen lines. Under the headline, 'The Murder of a Birmingham Police Constable', it said:

An inquest was held on Saturday afternoon at the Birmingham Police Court, on the body of Police Constable Lines, who died on Wednesday from injuries received in a street row on the 7th inst. Several witnesses swore that while Lines was endeavouring to effect the arrest of a burglar, Jeremiah Cockery, (sic) alias Corkoran, 22 years old, stabbed the constable behind the left ear. A verdict of wilful murder was returned against Cockery, who with eleven others is in custody. On being conveyed back to the gaol, Cockery sang, 'That's the sort of man I am;' and said to an officer, 'They have made it -------- hot for me; but it don't matter. About two minutes and it will be all over.'

And that was all that any newspaper reported on the murder until the trial in July.

The evidence was overwhelming that Jeremiah Corkery had stabbed PC Lines and when he appeared at the Warwick Assizes, the jury took only twenty minutes to convict him. On Tuesday, 27 July 1875, Corkery was hanged in Warwick Gaol.

There is something eerily modern about many aspects of the cases in this chapter; not least the astonishingly up-to-date language used.

Who could have imagined that in 1875, a man encouraging others to attack the police would have been shouting, 'Let's give it to the pigs!' or that in 1841, a crowd would be suggesting, apropos the police, that they should, 'Murder the bastards'?

Slowly but surely, attitudes changed and, by the 1880s, the public felt very differently about the murder of a police officer on duty. When Inspector Thomas Simmons was murdered in 1885, a crime which became known as 'The Romford Outrage', his funeral was a remarkable occasion. We saw earlier in this chapter that Robert Culley's funeral was marred by catcalls and abuse directed at the mourners, who included his pregnant wife. By 1885, the death on duty of a police officer was regarded very differently. The market town of Romford in Essex, where Inspector Simmons had served, virtually came to a halt for his funeral; a stark contrast to the funeral of PC Robert Culley some fifty years earlier. Thousands of ordinary people lined the streets of the funeral cortege and the outrage felt at Simmons' death was immense.

It took decades, but the citizens of Victorian Britain gradually came to see the police as their friends and protectors, rather than oppressors and agents of state control. The middle classes were the first to see the practical advantages of having a body of men around whose job was to look after their property and make sure that the streets were safe. The working class took a little longer to be convinced of the benefits of having a properly organized police force patrolling the cities and country roads, but by the 1880s it was widely accepted that the police were, by and large, a benefit to the community. There were still notoriously rough districts where a lone constable might be taking his life in his hands, were he to venture, but in most of the country, the sight of the police officer on patrol was a welcome and reassuring one.

Violent theft in the streets, more generally known as 'mugging', was a serious problem in the cities of mid-nineteenth-century Britain. It was regarded with consternation, precisely because respectable citizens had imperceptibly grown to rely upon the police to keep them safe when they were out late at night and the sudden discovery that ordinary people might be at risk of being attacked was a disconcerting one. Businessmen and shopkeepers might have objected to the establishment of regular police forces as being expensive and a curtailment of their liberties when first introduced in 1829, but it had taken only twenty years for them to get used to the idea. By 1851, when the wave of street robberies came to the public awareness, the question on everybody's lips was, 'What are the police doing about it?'

Chapter 3

The Garrotting Panic: Mugging and Street Robbery in Mid-nineteenth-century Britain

When we consider thefts in the street during the Victorian period, we naturally think of pickpockets. The image of the Artful Dodger from *Oliver Twist*, is a powerful and enduring one. That the streets of nineteenth-century cities such as Liverpool, Leeds and London were plagued with muggers, as well as pickpockets, may seem a strange idea. Even the expression, 'mugging', is surely a relatively recent importation from the United States? In fact, just as with the violent deaths of police officers in the course of civil disorder, mugging is a thoroughly British crime that has been practised in this country for centuries. Even the name of the crime has its origins in this country and was only decades later adopted by Americans to describe violent assaults in public places, followed by theft.

In 1851 and 1852, newspapers in Britain began to draw attention to a novel type of robbery, which came to be known as 'garrotting'. Three or four men would surround a pedestrian and while one pressed his arm round the victim's throat, choking him almost unconscious, the others would rifle through his pockets. This method of attack, involving pressure on the throat, might have been new, but robbing pedestrians was anything but a novelty. For centuries, groups of robbers had prowled the streets and outskirts of British cities, attacking lone travellers and stealing what they could from them. From the sixteenth century onwards, these men were known as footpads, to distinguish them from those robbers who rode horses and were known as highwaymen.

By the middle of the nineteenth-century, the word 'footpad' had an archaic and dated feel to it. The time was ripe for a new term to come into vogue to describe the activities of those who preyed on pedestrians in this way. That some victims were now being grabbed round the throat and deprived of breath in order to subdue them, suggested comparison with two foreign practices. One of these was the cult of Thuggee; followers of the goddess Kali, whose practices had recently been suppressed by the British authorities in India. These men were essentially bandits who waylaid travellers, strangling them and stealing their belongings. Thuggee entered the English language, but in a more general sense and contracted to 'thug', a word in common usage today. The word, which was eventually applied to those infesting the streets of the bigger cities and assaulting unwary people at night, was 'garrotters'. This derived from the traditional mode of capital punishment in Spain, the garrotte; which entailed choking the condemned person to death with a metal collar.

The reason this foreign word found its way into the English language was the result of a curious coincidence. At the time that these robberies involving strangulation began being reported in the newspapers, a news story from across the Atlantic broke in this country. A Venezuelan adventurer called Narciso Lopez had, with American backing, launched a guerrilla war in Cuba. When Lopez was captured in August 1851, the Spanish authorities in Cuba decided to make an example of him. For some reason, the account of Lopez' death captured the public's imagination in Britain. On 1 September 1851, the 54-year-old rebel leader was taken to a scaffold in the centre of Havana and tied to a metal chair. An iron collar was fastened around his neck and pulled tight with a lever, compressing the condemned man's windpipe and choking him to death. The garrotte had burst upon the British consciousness and provided a vernacular term for the wave of robberies taking place in cities from one end of the country to another.

An early report of such an offence set out clearly the way in which the 'garrotters' operated. On the night of 24 July 1852, a series of street robberies took place in the northern city of Leeds. *The Times* began their coverage of that Saturday night by asserting that, 'Garrotte robberies are increasing in number, violence and audacity in Leeds and its immediate vicinity …'

What had happened was that four young men had attacked two others on separate occasions during the same night and left them both in a very poor state. There was little doubt that the violence used was quite unnecessary and in addition to being choked unconscious, their victims had also been beaten around the head and left covered in blood. Those who had carried out these 'garrotte robberies' were captured with the proceeds of crime still in their possession.

Garrotting was especially prevalent in the north of England. Four months before the attacks in Leeds, a young man was murdered by garrotters in Hull. The body of F.W. Mablethorpe, a clerk, was discovered laying in the street near his home. He had been suffocated and his watch and money were missing. The dead man's face also bore other signs of violence, such as scratches and bruises. Ten days after the murder in Hull, there was another garrotting in Sheffield; another northern city. A prosperous businessman called Charles Henry Mort was seized from behind in the street and his throat constricted so that he could not cry out. A second man then went through his pockets, taking anything of value.

A curious point, which emerged during several trials of men accused of being garrotters, was that those carrying out such attacks did not themselves talk of 'garrotting', but used a word which will be familiar to any twenty-first century reader. When two men, George Roberts and Samuel Anderson, appeared at the Old Bailey on 24 November 1862, they were charged with violent theft and robbery. The press reported the case as that of two garrotters who had been caught and brought to justice. It was clear from the evidence that the two men had committed the crime with which they were charged: an attack on a medical student who was knocked down and robbed in central London. From that point of view, it was an unremarkable case. During the cross examination of one of the police officers though, an interesting fact came to light.

Sergeant William Good had arrested Roberts for the theft of a watch from the medical student who had been the victim of the two robbers. Roberts' response was to start swearing and fighting. He apparently said to Sergeant Good, 'You want me for putting the mug on, do you? I'll put the bloody mug on you!' There was a scuffle before the police officer was able to arrest Roberts. In the witness box, fearing perhaps that the court would not understand the thieves' jargon used in his evidence, Sergeant Good helpfully explained that, 'Mug' is slang used by thieves; it means garrotting.' Far from being some Americanism, which crossed the Atlantic to this country in the late 1960s, mugging was the term used for violent street robberies in Britain 150 years ago. It was the Americans who picked up the use of this word from us; not the other way round.

The response to the epidemic of mugging across Britain in the early 1850s was ferociously long sentences of imprisonment. When they were convicted of robbery, it turned out that both Roberts and Anderson had a string of previous convictions for various offences. Samuel Anderson was sent to prison for life and George Roberts got twenty years.

Despite the ruthlessness with which the courts treated those convicted of offences of this sort, there seemed no shortage of other young men ready to become garrotters. Newspaper headlines such as this, from *The Manchester Guardian* of 16 January 1857: 'DARING GAROTTE ROBBERY', or, 20 December 1854: 'GAROTTE ROBBERY AT MANCHESTER' were common for at least a decade between around 1851 and 1861. Before being brought to an abrupt halt by a change in the law.

At 1.00 am on Wednesday, 16 July 1862, Hugh Pilkington, the Liberal MP for Blackburn, was walking from a late sitting at the Commons to his home in St James'. His route took him through one of the wealthiest and most respectable parts of the capital; the avenue called Pall Mall, which runs from Trafalgar Square to Buckingham Palace. This was no dingy back street of a provincial city, but the very heart of the British Empire. Mr Pilkington must have felt utterly safe.

As he paused by the Reform Club, considering whether to visit it before going home to bed, two men rushed up and struck Pilkington round the head, knocking him to the ground. While one of the men gripped him by the throat, the other stole his pocket watch. They ran off before any of those who witnessed the attack had a chance to react. A short time earlier that evening, a very similar robbery had taken place in nearby Piccadilly, when a man was also knocked down and deprived of his watch. Both attacks were very quick and no money was stolen. The muggers evidently wanted to move fast, secure a valuable watch and then make off, rather than spend time searching the pockets of their victims; so increasing the risk of being caught.

The mugging of an MP in the middle of the West End caused huge concern in Parliament. It was one thing for such crimes to take place in Leeds or Hull; quite another to see it happening within sight of Buckingham Palace. There have, in recent years, been suggestions that the fear of muggers at this time was really no more than a 'Moral Panic', whipped up and incited by the press. It is true that newspapers were quick to publicize the mugging of an MP in the heart of London, but they can hardly be blamed for street robberies becoming common. It might be the case that *The Times*, for example, took more interest in street robberies after the mugging of an MP, but that such offences were being committed was indisputable. At 10.00 pm on the Sunday night after the attack on Hugh Pilkington, a man called David Cameron got off a train at London Bridge station. As he left the station, three men surrounded him and while one grabbed hold of him, the other two stole his watch. A few days later, George Lewis, the young man who had robbed David Cameron, attacked and robbed a hatter called Francis Judd. It is quite true that such cases did not excite the same outrage as the mugging of an MP, but street robbery had definitely become a problem.

At least poor Hugh Pilkington had the satisfaction of seeing his unfortunate experience immortalized in literature. *Phineas Finn*, the second of Anthony Trollope's 'Palliser' novelsm was published in *St Paul's Magazine* through 1867 and 1868. The eponymous hero of the novel becomes an MP and is walking home from a sitting at the House of Commons, with a fellow Member of Parliament, Robert Kennedy. They part near Grosvenor Square, but Finn glances back and sees that:

> *Mr. Kennedy did not reach the corner. When he was within two doors of it, one of the men had followed him up quickly, and had thrown something round his throat from behind him. Phineas understood well now that his friend was in the act of being garrotted, and that his instant assistance was needed. He rushed forward, and as the second ruffian had been close upon the footsteps of the first, there was almost instantaneously a concourse of the four men. But there was no fight. The man who had already nearly succeeded in putting Mr. Kennedy on to his back, made no attempt to seize his prey when he found that so unwelcome an addition had joined the party, but instantly turned to fly.*

This scene, inspired by Pilkington's mugging, is a pivotal point in the book and leads to the protagonist being brought into the government.

Trollope wasn't the only writer using garrotting as a theme in the 1850s and 1860s. In the spring of 1857 a farce called *Anti-Garrotte*, by C.J. Collins, was staged at the Adelphi and songs and cartoons about garrotting appeared in many places; most notably *Punch* magazine. The motif of violent robbers waylaying victims in the street was also used in many novels.

In recent years, there have been periodic complaints about the fact that criminals do not serve the full term of imprisonment to which the courts have sentenced them. Instead, they are released early; sometimes they go on to commit other crimes. Every so often, there will be a particularly dreadful case of a criminal who has been released after serving only half the sentence imposed and who then carries out a precisely similar crime to that for which he was originally imprisoned. This, too, is no new phenomenon. Transportation to Australia as a punishment declined sharply during the 1840s. At the height of transportations in 1833, almost 7,000 people a year were shipped off to the colonies; fifteen years later, the number had dropped to around a third of that and by 1853, the practice more or less came to an end.

From the early 1850s, with transportation no longer an option, the only way of dealing with non-capital offences was, by and large, imprisonment. The prisons soon became clogged up with men serving long sentences; it not being uncommon to give a man fifteen or twenty years hard labour, often simply because he was a repeat offender. Housing and feeding all these men was a nuisance and so in 1853, long-serving prisoners became eligible for early release, after they had served a certain proportion of their sentence; provided that they had behaved themselves in prison. Such individuals were known as 'Ticket-of-Leave men'

Human nature being what it is, it was inevitable that some of these paroled prisoners would commit further offences, as soon as they were released. The rumour circulated that the garrotting epidemic was being fuelled by 'Ticket-of-Leave men' and that it was softness on the part of the authorities which was causing a rise in violent crime. This belief was prompted in part because the law, which allowed for the early discharge of prisoners from their sentences, the *Penal Servitude Act 1853*, came into force at the very time that garrotting was on the rise and transportation to Australia was coming to an end.

The complaints about prisoners being released early and then committing further offences have a particularly modern feel to them. Headlines in the newspapers would often include cases of 'garrotters' and 'Ticket-of-Leave men' together; as though to suggest that the two types were more or less interchangeable.

Before considering the steps taken to deal with the epidemic of mugging, it is worth asking what had precipitated such brutal crimes in the first place and how the activities of the garrotters were viewed by ordinary, respectable citizens.

The nineteenth-century saw the exponential growth of British cities. At the beginning of the century, for instance, there were just over a million people living in London. By 1900, the city's population had risen to six and a half million. Some of this increase was fuelled by the natural growth in population, which took place over the century, but much was due to the migration of people from the countryside to the cities; a consequence of the Industrial Revolution. In 1801, fewer than 10 per cent of people in England and Wales were living in cities with 100,000 or more inhabitants; by 1901, the figure was 35 per cent. The inexorable rise in urban living caused many problems, not least those relating to law and order.

When poor people lived in a village, most of their neighbours and the people they see from day to day were likely to be in a similar condition. The wealthy lived in large houses, and encounters with the gentry by ordinary agricultural workers were often limited to brief glimpses as coaches or riders passed by. In cities, the case was quite different. Although the working classes tended to live in separate districts, they rubbed shoulders with the well-to-do on the streets and saw every day that many of those living in the city were doing far better than they were themselves. The wealthy streets were highly visible and the way of life for those who were much richer than they were themselves was on constant display. Inevitably, these regular reminders of their own inferior status in the scheme of things generated envy and resentment.

There must have been a great temptation to redress the inequalities a little by simply grabbing watches and taking the money of those who were doing so much better than themselves. The anonymous streets of a big city provided a perfect hunting ground for those wishing to strike at their social superiors in this way.

Then, as now, the muggers and their victims almost invariably came from different social classes, and the crimes themselves were generally committed in areas some way from where the mugger himself lived. The street robbers often travelled from the poorer districts into the centres of cities, in order to prey on those who were well dressed; a *modus operandi* which is still frequently followed to this day by muggers. It was not merely theft, but specifically theft from social superiors; a primitive means of redistributing the wealth of society.

What of the victims of these robberies? How did they view the depredations of the garrotters? It is curious to note that although twenty years earlier, many of these respectable people regarded the establishment of police forces as being a step along the road to tyranny, they had by now grown used to having their property and persons protected by the police. The realization that they were now at the mercy of thieves and robbers and that it was only the police who stood between them and the violence of the garrotters was a sobering one. They had become accustomed to reading in the newspapers about police officers being the victims of savage and sometimes deadly assaults on the streets; it seemed now that they themselves were on the front line. They demanded action.

There can be no doubt that the mugging of an MP in the very centre of the capital acted as a catalyst for what happened next. It is altogether possible that any number respectable businessmen and shopkeepers in Leeds and Sheffield might have been half strangled as they walked home late at night, without Parliament moving as swiftly as it did when one of its own members fell victim to the crime wave. At any rate, the loss of Hugh Pilkington's watch was to set in motion a sequence of events which reduced street robberies to a manageable level practically overnight.

The year after the mugging of the member for Blackburn, Parliament voted through a new bill; one designed to put an end to violent street robberies. This was the *Security of the Persons of her Majesty's Subjects from Personal Violence Bill*; which, when passed, became more commonly known as the *Security from Violence Act of 1863*. Even this was a bit of a mouthful and most people knew it simply as the 'Garrotters Act'. The existing penalties for theft with violence were already very harsh. The prospect of lengthy sentences did not appear to deter certain aggressive young men from trying their luck at street robbery.

Until 1863, those arrested for mugging were charged under either Section 21 of the *Offences Against the Person Act* or Section 43 of the *Larceny Act*. In both cases, the maximum punishment was a term of imprisonment with hard labour. Under the Garrotters Act, robbery with violence could now be punished with up to fifty strokes of the 'cat-o'-nine-tails'.

The 'cat' had been used by the British Army and Navy for years. It consisted of a wooden handle, 19 inches long, to which were attached nine 'tails' of whipcord, bound at the ends with silk thread. These tails were 33 inches long. The cat o' nine tails was applied to the bare back of the victim and caused a tremendous amount of pain. Under the provisions of the Garrotters Act, up to fifty strokes could be awarded; to be inflicted before the convicted man was sent to prison.

The flogging was undertaken by stripping the prisoner to the waist and strapping him to a wooden frame. The legs were securely fastened and the man's arms stretched above his head. A prison officer, who was paid extra for the job, would then administer the required number of lashes. A doctor was always in attendance and could stop the punishment at any time, if he thought that the man's life was in danger. Soon after the new law reached the statute book, a youth of nineteen was convicted of a particularly brutal robbery in Liverpool and sentenced to fifty strokes of the cat, to be followed by four years hard labour. The doctor on duty during the flogging checked the young man's breathing and pulse at intervals and after thirty-six strokes, ordered the punishment to be ended. He felt that there was a genuine risk of permanent injury, or even death, if the full fifty lashes were to be inflicted.

Another eyewitness account is given by a journalist of the flogging of two men in Yorkshire, who had been convicted of garotte robberies following the passage of the so-called 'Garotters Act'. This punishment took place on 17 January 1867.

Yesterday afternoon two men who had been convicted at the Leeds gaol delivery of garotte robberies, and sentenced by Mr Justice Lush to receive two dozen strokes of the cat-o'-nine-tails each, in addition to penal servitude, underwent the flogging in the central hall of the gaol.

The delinquent first fastened to the triangle was Thomas Beaumont, aged 47, who had been sentenced to five years penal servitude for garrotting Abraham Dickenson at Batley, near Dewsbury. The 'cat' was a new one, which bore, at the end of the handle, the seal of the Home Office.

The length of the lashes was nearly a yard, and at the extremity of each one were three hard knots.

The prisoner was fastened to the triangle by straps at ankles, knees, and hands and a leather band was placed round the neck to prevent the lash hitting the victim in that part of the body. The 'operators' upon the occasion were two warders of the gaol, who administered in each instance a dozen strokes in succession.

Beaumont received the first stroke in silence, but the second extorted from him an exclamation of pain, and at the third he cried aloud "Oh dear me". At the fifth cut he writhed a good deal, and at the tenth showed that he was undergoing intense agony. After the twelfth stroke, and while the 'cat' was being transferred to a more rapid executioner, the naked back was seen to present plain marks of the severity of the castigation. The blows given by the new whipper fell more rapidly than those which preceded, and the whole of Beaumont's punishment was completed in about a minute and a half. He was then released from the triangle and taken back to his cell in an exhausted state. The laceration of the flesh was obvious enough, and the 'weals' might easily have been counted.

The man next brought out for corporal punishment was a low set but muscular young man named Michael Guirtay, who had been sentenced to penal servitude for ten years for a garrotte robbery at Bradford. He was out on a ticket-of-leave when he committed this offence, having all his life been in prison. At his trial the judge said that he had been committed no less than fifteen times, and his last sentence was five years' penal servitude.

The first descent of the whip made him cry "Oh," in a piteous tone, and at the second he cried out "Oh dear," after the fourth he begged for and was given a glass of water; and at the ninth, he resisted so strongly, though without the least avail, that the framework to which he was bound was moved slightly from its original starting point. As the blows followed each other in quick succession his cries of suffering were louder and more frequent. It was in vain that he asked for mercy, or, in a dreadful paroxysm of pain, promised that he would "never do so again." A cessation of his howling showed that the flogging had been duly inflicted "according to the law" and he was taken away apparently in a stronger state than the wretched man who had preceded him. His back was more cut up than that of Beaumont had been, and, though no blood followed the strokes in either case, there was sufficient evidences in both of the severity of the chastisement.

The surgeon of the gaol (Mr W.N. Price), and, Mr Keene, the governor, superintended the castigation. Eight or nine of the 369 inmates of the gaol, who had been refractory, were purposely made spectators of what passed, with a view to deterring them from lawless acts, for which the visiting justices have the power to order the use of the whip.

This account of the punishments meted out to garrotters makes grim reading today. Incredibly, the 'cat' was still being used in British prisons well into the 1950s and was last awarded in 1962.

After the attack on Hugh Pilkington, the police in London had done their best both to reduce the actual number of muggings, by increasing the number of patrols, and also to try and make it look as though offences were falling by massaging the figures a little. Areas where the garrotters were known to operate were flooded with officers, and it was made clear to the criminal fraternity that this was a type of crime which would bring down the most condign punishment upon those engaging in it. It was when the bill which allowed flogging for street robberies began moving through Parliament that the actual number of robberies began to drop though, and when the Garrotters Act became law, the numbers plummeted dramatically. In 1863, the year that the Garotters Act became law, there were sixty convictions for street robberies involving violence. The following year, despite intensified police action against the garotters, this figure had dropped to forty-three; a decline of 33 per cent in one year. There was every indication that whereas the most savage prison sentences did nothing to discourage muggers; the prospect of a flogging made them think twice.

The statistics for robbery with violence in the year following the passing of the Garotters Act make interesting reading. In the course of those twelve months, nineteen men were flogged under the provisions of the act; only four of whom were punished in London. Of the others, four each were flogged in Birmingham and Leeds, three in Liverpool, two in Durham and one each in Salford and Reading. It was clear that garrotting was a nationwide phenomenon and not merely restricted to the capital.

While the police across London cracked down on the gangs carrying out such attacks following the mugging of Pilkington, a similar thing happened in provincial cities, as the newspapers drew attention to the fact that it was becoming unsafe to walk home late at night.

The prevalence of street robbery fluctuated greatly throughout the Victorian period. At one time, it was a common offence and anybody walking home at night could fear muggers or garrotters. At others times there were crackdowns by the police and the courts; with savage sentences of twenty years or more for a single offence. These police actions, combined with tough and well-publicized punishments handed out by the courts, certainly acted to discourage such crimes, if only temporarily. The Garrotters Act had a similar effect.

The garrotting panic illustrates the great change in how police were viewed by the upper and middle classes in Victorian Britain. They had stopped being a 'bogyman' or agent of repressive government to respectable citizens and instead were seen as their protector. The anger about street robberies was directed not only against the cowardly thugs committing the offences, but also against the police for not preventing them. Imperceptibly, over the decades since PC Robert Culley's death, ordinary people had become accustomed to the idea that the police were there for their own good and that keeping the streets safe could be left to the police. It was the perception that the streets of cities as far apart as Liverpool and Leeds, London and Sheffield were no longer safe to walk after dark, which caused anxiety and led those who might once have had reservations about the very idea of a regular police force, instead to embrace the idea enthusiastically.

It is interesting that then, as now, these crimes were seen by the perpetrators as striking back at an unjust and unequal social system. The mugger, like the rioter, came almost invariably from the lower strata and his victims were usually well-dressed men and women from a superior social class. Those who took part in garrotte robberies were uneducated and usually unemployed men, whose prospects in nineteenth-century Britain were frightful. There was no social security, no benefits system, NHS or welfare state. Those without work could, and did, starve. Without even the right to vote, the ordinary working-class person was in no position to try to change the system.

Acts of violence towards figures of authority and the garrotting and mugging of the well-to-do were committed by the direct inheritors of the tradition, which led to such wild scenes as the Gordon Riots of 1780. Without any sort of stake in the political system or social order, on the fringes of society, eking out a living; such people had little to lose. Rioting and acts of violence on the streets were perhaps the only way the average person in Britain could express their feelings in the early years of Victoria's reign. Even prison was not such a terrifying prospect, at least there would be no chance of starving there; a very real and present danger in the outside world.

The police were not always able to cope with incidents of civil unrest and sometimes fell back on the time-honoured expedient of calling for help from the armed forces. The regularity with which the military was used to suppress riots, strikes and discontent is a little disconcerting Nevertheless, it is the fact that at various times in this period, whole swathes of England and Wales were effectively under martial law. In the summer of 1842, for instance, Lancashire and Yorkshire were effectively under the control of the military, and industrial cities like Sheffield and Halifax had bodies of troops quartered in and around them for considerable periods of time.

Chapter 4

Calling Out the Military: The Use of Troops to Suppress Disorder and Rioting

The idea of the army being used in this country to tackle rioters is regarded with universal repugnance. So used are we to being able to depend upon a largely unarmed police force to maintain order in the streets, that the very thought of troops taking over this function fills us with horror. When it was suggested, during the wave of rioting in England in 2011, that the armed forces might be brought in to aid the civil power, there was outrage; not least from the police who were tackling the riots. Tim Godwin, acting head of the Metropolitan Police, clashed publicly with Prime Minister David Cameron when the latter floated the notion that using troops to deal with the rioting was one option being considered So fixed and determined is the public view of this matter, that it would be little short of political suicide for any government to call in the military. All else apart, it would be an admission of failure; a sign that civil society had reached the lowest point imaginable. It was not always so.

Until shortly before the beginning of Queen Victoria's reign the army was the not the last resort, but the first response to any sort of disorder; from drunken apprentices to striking workers. With no established police force, only the military had the manpower and weapons necessary to restore calm. This was all well and good in the kind of agrarian society that existed in Britain before the Industrial Revolution. A crowd of angry peasants roaming the countryside might very well be dispersed by the cavalry. Things changed, though, when the majority of the population moved into cities. An army commander could give his men a free hand to behave as savagely as they wished in fields and woods; but when operating in the streets of a city, cavalry charges are seldom a good idea. Even volleys of fire over the heads of a crowd are liable to kill respectable citizens looking out of their bedroom windows. It was, among other things, the use of cavalry during the 'Peterloo Massacre' in Manchester in 1819, which caused those in authority to think seriously about replacing soldiers as the chief means of keeping the peace with an effective police force. During the political meeting at St Peter's Fields in 1819, cavalry were used to disperse the peaceful crowds, which resulted in hundreds of casualties. Troopers rode down women and children and then hacked at them with their sabres. This was seen, even at the time, as being a far from desirable way of maintaining order in cities.

It took a century or so before the British police were truly able to fulfil this function of maintaining the peace. They had certainly not done so by the end of Victoria's reign in 1901.

What has been called 'The Last Battle on English Soil' took place a year after Victoria became queen and only a few weeks before her coronation in 1838. This 'battle' was with no foreign invader, but was fought between ordinary English agricultural workers and soldiers of the British Army. In its way, the Battle of Bossenden Wood was a watershed; marking the end of reliance upon the army alone to deal with unrest and pointing the way to the need for efficient police forces in every part of Britain.

John Nichols Thom was a wine dealer from Cornwall. He was mentally unstable and had spent four years in an asylum, before settling near Canterbury in Kent. He began calling himself, 'Sir William Courtney' and set out to build a following among the farm labourers in the district. Dressing in a variety of exotic costumes, ranging from that of a general to something resembling the sort of outfit which might have been worn by an Oriental potentate, the self-styled 'Sir William' hinted that his secret identity was none other than that of the messiah and that he had come to usher in the millennium; that time foretold in the Bible, when the meek would inherit the Earth. This was welcome news for the impoverished and disenfranchized country folk and 'Sir William' became immensely popular. He was certainly not entirely sane and perhaps he began to believe his own stories, because on Monday, 28 May 1838, he led a few of his faithful up and down the countryside around Canterbury, collecting followers who seemed to accept him as Christ. Some of those he lured from their work were employed by local farmers, who applied to a magistrate to take some action to prevent the nuisance developing further. The magistrate issued a warrant for Sir William Courtney's arrest and this was given to the parish constable to serve.

Nicholas Mears, the constable for the district, was probably capable enough when it came to keeping an eye on poachers and controlling cheeky boys, but handling what was looking increasingly like a religiously inspired insurrection certainly took him way out of his depth. On the morning of Thursday, 31 May, accompanied by his brother, Nicholas Mears arrived at the farm where Sir William Courtney and his disciples were camped and attempted to arrest him. The wanted man drew a pistol and shot dead the constable on the spot. The murdered man's brother fled, following which the self-proclaimed messiah mutilated the corpse of the constable with a sword.

This left a band of fewer than fifty men roaming the countryside. All but two of these men were armed with nothing more fearsome than sticks and knives. It was precisely the sort of situation which called for the services of a well-organized and effective police force. Instead, the local magistrates swore in a number of special constables. These volunteers were precisely analogous to a posse in the Wild West. Some approached Bossendon Wood, where Sir William Courtney and his men were hiding out, and fired their shotguns at them. It was plain that nobody really knew what to do next and so a message was sent to Canterbury, calling for military assistance. A hundred men of the

45th Regiment of Foot were despatched, under the command of four officers; Major Armstrong and three lieutenants.

The troops were split into three groups and approached the men hiding in the woods from different directions. One of the parties was under the command of Lieutenant Henry Bennett. He tried to avoid bloodshed by walking within a short distance of the group in Bossendon Wood and calling on them to surrender. Sir William Courtney shot him dead. At this point, Bennett's men took matters into their own hands and opened fire; killing ten men, including Sir William Courtney himself. One of those shot dead was George Catt, a special constable who was caught in the crossfire. A number of men were wounded by the gunfire, whereupon the rebels all surrendered.

The courts were surprisingly lenient with those who took part in this episode. A dozen men were sentenced to death for the murder of Lieutenant Bennett and the constable who had been sent to arrest Sir William Courtney in the first place. All the sentences were commuted though, with two men transported for life, one for ten years and the remainder given only one year's imprisonment.

At the time of the Battle of Bossenden Wood, and for some while afterwards, most parts of Britain continued in the old and largely ineffective way of having parish constables and enlisting the help of volunteer special constables on an *ad hoc* basis, when things looked as though they might be getting out of hand. And, of course, the army was always able to lend a hand when things became too dangerous or disorderly.

The 45th Regiment of Foot, the unit which took part in the Battle of Bossendon Wood, was in action a year later; this time in Wales. In the summer of 1839, the Chartist movement was on the rise. The name 'Chartism' came from the six point People's Charter to which members subscribed. Four of their demands have long been accepted; not only in this country but in almost every true democracy. The Chartists wanted votes for all adult men, secret ballots, payment of

MPs, no property qualification to be necessary to stand for parliament, equal constituencies and annual general elections. Annual parliaments would not be practical and completely equal constituencies hard to achieve, but by and large, the People's Charter strikes us today as a moderate enough programme. In a nation where even a demonstration calling for the rights of working-class people to be respected was seen as outrageous and likely to lead to chaos and revolution, the Chartists were viewed by the establishment with great suspicion.

Because there was little chance of constitutionally achieved change, bearing in mind that almost 95 per cent of adults had no vote at this time, some of the Chartists decided that they were justified in more direct action. This was to take the form of simultaneous 'risings' across the whole of Britain. The aim of this action was to seize a number of cities and even entire rural districts and wrest them from control of the government in Westminster. These days we have MI5, Special Branch and so on to counter such threats, but with large parts of Britain lacking any sort of organized police force, it inevitably fell to the army to tackle the extremists.

In July 1839 came preliminary skirmishes, which demonstrated that a well-organized police force was capable of dealing with subversion and disorder. The Chartist convention met in Birmingham and held several open-air meetings where speakers publicly announced their dissatisfaction with the political system. Birmingham had at that time no police force of its own, being reliant upon a couple of dozen 'street keepers', most of whom were elderly. At the request of the Home Office, who were concerned about the possibility of some sort of insurrection in the city, the Metropolitan Police sent sixty officers to Birmingham by train and as soon as they arrived, they rushed to the Bull Ring in the centre of the town and attempted to clear the area.

The size of the meeting being held in the centre of Birmingham, and the inflammatory nature of the speeches being made were bad enough, but it was also observed that many members of the crowd were armed with bludgeons, pieces of wood, iron railings and other weapons. When the Metropolitan Police tried to break up the meetings, a riot began. The police were taken aback by the ferocity of the opposition which they faced and fell back in disorder. Three officers were stabbed and many others injured after being struck by bits of metal, half bricks and stones.

The problem was not that a force of ordinary police could not have controlled such a demonstration, it was that they had been marched straight into action without being given a chance to formulate a plan of action. As it was, the army had to assist them in restoring order. The 4th Irish Dragoons and the Rifle Brigade moved in to the Bull Ring, whereupon the crowd fled.

The police officers from London remained in Birmingham and when trouble erupted again, they were more ready for it than they had been on that first occasion. There were more disturbances, including the burning down of houses and shops, but the police adopted an aggressive and proactive stance, charging at the first sign of trouble. The magistrates in Birmingham were able to see for themselves that a well-organized police force could deal with almost anything in the way of civil disorder.

On 24 July, the government announced that £10,000 was to be made available from the Treasury to enable the authorities in Birmingham to set up their own police force; which was to be modelled on the Metropolitan Police. It had taken serious rioting to show the advantages of having a regular police force in the city. There were those who accused the police of brutality in the way that they dispersed the Chartist demonstrations in Birmingham that July, but three months later, it became clear what could have happened, had no action been taken to break up the gatherings in Birmingham.

In the autumn of 1839, some of the more militant Chartists hatched a plan to take over the part of South Wales which surrounded Newport and Cardiff and declare a republic. By any definition, this can only be regarded as at best treason and at worst, an attempt to start a civil war. The rising was to begin in the town of Newport and once that had been taken, was to spread from there to other parts of South Wales and then, it was hoped, perhaps the whole of Britain. Tentative plans had been made in other locations, such as the West Riding of Yorkshire, and even the East End of London, for uprisings to take place there as well.

The original scheme for Newport had been to attack the town by night, but a combination of ineptitude on the part of the plotters, combined with poor weather, meant that the column of Chartists did not reach Newport until after dawn on 4 November 1839. Some of their comrades had already been arrested in the town and were held at the Westgate Hotel. It is impossible to say at this late date, just how many men were involved in the attack on Newport; which was the last armed uprising to take place in Britain. Certainly there were some thousands. Most were armed only with pikes and spears, although a few carried shotguns and pistols. The authorities caught wind of the attacks and enrolled a number of special constables. More to the point, they had almost 100 soldiers at their disposal. Of these, sixty were already stationed in the town and reinforcements of thirty two members of the 45th Regiment of Foot reached Newport a short time before the rebels.

With somewhere in the region of 3,000 to 5,000 men facing them, the small squad of soldiers thought it tactically wise to establish a defensible position. The soldiers chose the Westgate Hotel, where the prisoners already captured were held. Perhaps the attacking force of Chartists thought that with the sheer weight of numbers on their side, a frontal assault on the hotel would be sure to over-run the defenders, because the thousands of men who had marched into Newport that morning simply made straight for the Westgate Hotel and began attacking it. The troops within were all equipped with muskets and had sufficient powder and shot that they would have been able to withstand an assault by anybody, never mind a ragtag mob of colliery workers carrying improvised spears. It was sheer slaughter, with the soldiers firing volley after volley into the crowds besieging the hotel. One or two men managed to climb through windows at the rear of the building and they too were shot down as soon as they were spotted.

It is interesting to note that this whole affair was, despite the political overtones, really just another 'freedom riot'; the focus of the crowd was, essentially, freeing imprisoned friends rather than overthrowing the government.

The true casualty figures for the Newport Rising will never be known, because many of those wounded and killed were simply taken home. What is certain is that at least twenty-four people died of bullet wounds that day and fifty more were seriously injured. There were no casualties among the soldiers in the hotel.

The government was horrified at this abortive revolution and mass arrests were made. Many of those arrested were charged with relatively minor public order offences but twenty-one were charged with high treason; which in this case consisted in levying war on the monarch in her realm. Three of the ringleaders of the affair, John Frost, William Jones and Zephaniah Williams, were found guilty of high treason and became a minor footnote in judicial history at the Monmouth Shire Hall on 16 January 1840, when they were sentenced to be hung, drawn and quartered; the last such sentence ever to be delivered in this country. Even as the judge spoke the dreadful formula though, he knew that there was no chance of such a procedure being carried out. The sentences on all three men were commuted to transportation for life.

It was believed that the rising in Newport was to be the signal for other actions in places as far apart as Sheffield, Bradford and London. The uprising which was planned for the East End of London was dealt with most easily of them all, because, of course, the Metropolitan Police were on the scene to prevent the large scale disturbances, which were supposed to provide the opening shots of the campaign to set up a republic in England.

The value of having a permanent police force in every city and rural district was slowly coming to be appreciated by authorities throughout Britain. Even after the events in Birmingham and Newport, though, some districts resisted the setting up of their own forces, preferring to do the job on the cheap with the old and inefficient system of watchmen and parish constables. Even these authorities changed their minds after the General Strike of 1842.

The very expression, 'The General Strike of 1842', sounds a little odd. Surely, the 'General Strike' took place in 1926? To understand what led up to the strike of 1842, we need to look at the situation in the north of England in the years between 1839 and 1841. This was a time of great hardship and misery, particularly in the manufacturing districts of Yorkshire and Staffordshire. A major cause of this was the *Poor Law Amendment Act* of 1834. Until then, the Speenhamland System had been operating. This was a rudimentary form of supplementary benefits; paid in cash to people whose income fell below a certain level. It meant that a farm worker could obtain a regular sum of cash to supplement his wages and ensure that he and his family had enough to eat. It was similar in some ways to the modern system of tax credits.

Because it was seen as wasteful, inefficient and expensive, the Speenhamland System was abolished in 1834 and from then on, the only assistance given to the poor was admission to the workhouse. In these institutions, families were split up and the inmates were forced to wear degrading uniforms as though they were prisoners. Many people preferred starvation in their own homes to going into the workhouse and the overall effect, particularly in the provinces, was to create a sense of injustice which turned into a hatred of the authorities. This hatred manifested itself in strikes, rioting and sabotage, which was put down by the use of the army. The army, on the whole, tended to dislike being used for peacekeeping duties of this sort in their own country.

From 1839 to 1841, General Sir Charles Napier was in charge, overall, of the army in the North of England. His letters show what he and other senior officers felt about the situation and the duties they were expected to undertake. Writing to his brother, Colonel William Napier, on 19 January 1840, the general had this to say:

> *Misery is running riot through the greatest part of this district, that is to say through the manufacturing parts ... the poor here have resolved to die rather than go into the Union Houses. At Sheffield, not a man faced the Dragoons; fire and assassination are their weapons, and now their nature, because they are driven to that course, the poor law being the goad to keep them going ... The hatred of this law is not confined to Chartists, nor to the poor, it creates Chartists, it makes them sanguinary; they mean to spare no one who has a good coat if once they get to work: in short it is all hell, or likely to be so soon in England.*

There are a number of interesting points about this letter; not least, the astonishing sympathy which an army general displays for the poor of northern England. When Napier says of the 'sanguinary' or bloodthirsty agitators, that 'they mean to spare no one who has a good coat if once they get to work', he is echoing the thesis, that such disturbances had deeper causes than the ostensible reasons for the unrest; in this case, the level of wages. There was a general resentment against those who 'had good coats', by those who barely had enough food for their children.

The year of William IV's death and Victoria's accession to the throne in 1837, coincidentally marked the beginning of a recession which hit industrial workers especially severely. Employers tried to cut costs by reducing wages and putting workers on part time. This meant that the families of coal miners, factory workers and others faced the prospect of being forced into the workhouse through no fault of their own.

As Charles Napier observed, many would rather die than go into the workhouse and so the struggle between the employees and employers became, quite literally, a matter of life and death.

Matters came to a head in the summer of 1842, when miners in Staffordshire went on strike for shorter hours and an increase in wages. From Staffordshire, strikes spread outwards into Lancashire, Yorkshire and then to South Wales, Scotland and as far south as Cornwall. Eventually, that summer, over half a million workers were striking; the most serious industrial action to take place in nineteenth-century Britain.

The reason that we do not hear about the great General Strike of 1842 is that a brilliant piece of propaganda by the factory owners and government transformed the enterprise into a faintly ridiculous sounding affair. One way of closing down a factory was a form of sabotage which entailed draining the boilers of the steam engines operating the machinery. The easiest way of achieving this end was by removing the plugs and letting the water run out. Once this was done, the factories depending upon steam engines were effectively crippled. The name by which history remembers the General Strike is the trivial and absurd sounding 'Plug Plot Riots'.

It was in the north of England that the most bitter confrontations took place between strikers and the army. As mills and mines were closed down by the strike, large bodies of strikers, numbering according to some estimates over 50,000 strong, moved from town to town, doing their best to get others to join the strike. Apart from the vested interest of the factory owners in preventing more men and women coming out on strike, there was the undeniable fact that some of these large crowds were becoming menacing and beginning to engage in looting and intimidation. On 12 August 1842, cotton factories in the Lancashire town of Preston were hit by a strike. Those who walked out then toured the town, encouraging other mills and businesses to close. The following day, the strikers gathered again in the town at first light and visited factories where the workers had not yet joined the strike. Windows were broken, men were threatened and by 8.00 am, the local mayor, Samuel Horrocks, had had enough. He mustered a force of police and summoned a body of soldiers; men of the 72nd Highlanders, commanded by a Captain Woodford.

Although there exist no unbiased accounts of what happened next, it is agreed that the Riot Act was read and the crowd called upon to disperse. Far from leaving the centre of Preston, they began to jeer and throw stones at the mayor. When the police tried to act, there was strong resistance, with officers being struck with sticks and hit by stones. At this point, the order was given by the magistrate for the troops to open fire on the strikers. The results were shocking, with at least a dozen people falling to the ground with bullet wounds. One man had his kneecap blown off and needed to have his leg amputated as a result. Worse still, four of the men were killed. They were John Mercer, aged twenty-seven, William Lancaster, twenty-five, George Sowerbutts, nineteen and finally 17-year-old Bernard McNamara.

Later that day, the 72nd Highlanders were marched out of Preston and replaced with units from the Rifle Brigade. Preston might have been cowed by the shootings, but in neighbouring Yorkshire things were as bad as ever.

The day after the Preston shootings, there was a huge meeting of strikers on Bradford Moor. On Monday, 15 August, these men and women made their way towards Halifax, while others converged on the town from Todmorden. The magistrate in Halifax, Mr J.W. Hird, panicked and called for the help of not only the infantry, but also a cavalry regiment of hussars. There were a number of skirmishes and prisoners were taken by the soldiers. The next day, these men were due to be transferred to Wakefield Prison. On Tuesday, 16 August the situation worsened to such an extent that, for a while, it looked as though insurgents might be on the point of taking over the town of Halifax.

The authorities proposed to take the prisoners by train to Wakefield. Two ordinary, horse-drawn buses were obtained, and the prisoners placed in them with their police escorts. As they travelled to the station, accompanied by police escorts and a cavalry troop, things began to unravel in the most deadly way. The route to the station led past a hill called Salter-Hebble Hill and, unknown to the police and soldiers, an ambush was planned for this point. As the prisoners' buses approached the hill, a force of 3,000 or so men charged towards them. There were only thirteen hussars and they were quickly overwhelmed by this sudden rush. Some of the soldiers were dragged from their horses and their weapons seized. The buses were stoned, the windows broken and the rest of the cavalry put to flight. It was an ignominious defeat for a body of professional soldiers. Again, this ambush has the motif of 'freedom riot', in which the greatest determination of angry crowds is the release of their comrades, rather than any more general aim, such as the launching of a revolution.

This victory against the army plainly gave the strikers a sense of invulnerability, because later that day they surged into Halifax and attacked a mill owned by a man called Ackroyd. This time, the soldiers who faced them were prepared. After the Riot Act had been read and they had failed to leave the area, the troops opened fire, killing three men. These were not the only deaths to take place during the General Strike. Three men were shot dead by the army in Blackburn and another in Burslem.

The actions taken by the authorities that summer and the consequent deaths that underlined the need for maintaining proper police forces, persuaded counties like Staffordshire to establish their own force. It often took serious disorder to persuade counties and cities to establish a police force. In addition to suspicion and resentment of the newly established police forces by the working class, there was the issue of local authorities being reluctant to set up police forces in the districts for which they were responsible. There were two chief reasons for this.

The first was that, having been accustomed to being independent in the matter of law enforcement, counties and boroughs did not really want the government in London dictating to them what they should be doing. The second reason for opposition was purely economic: setting up a proper, paid police force was expensive. While the army was financed directly by the government in London and cost nothing to those calling upon the military for assistance, a police force would have to be paid for by increasing rates (the predecessor of the modern Council Tax), always a very unpopular move with the electorate.

In the end, this reluctance to establish proper police forces was overcome by the passing of the *1856 County and Borough Police Act*, which obliged all boroughs and counties to have their own police force. To ensure that the act was complied with, provision was made for independent inspection of the police.

The greatly differing attitudes to the use of soldiers for crowd control in the provinces, as opposed to the capital, is very neatly illustrated by what became known as the 'Reform Riots' or 'Hyde Park Railings Affair', which took place in Hyde Park, twenty-four years after the General Strike.

Hyde Park is world famous for its Speakers' Corner, where anybody may deliver lectures and speeches on any subject which takes their fancy. The police stand by as ardent socialists preach revolution and the overthrow of the monarchy, while others denounce western society in general and call for the setting up of an Islamic state. It was not always so. In 1866, there was political agitation throughout the whole country for a reform in the franchise; the right to vote. In July of that year, one of the groups pressing for change announced their intention to hold a rally in Hyde Park on the evening of Monday, 23 July. At the instigation of the Home Secretary, Commissioner of Police for the Metropolis Sir Richard Mayne issued an order forbidding this meeting. When Lord Melbourne took a similarly high-handed approach back in 1833, it resulted in rioting and the death of a police officer in Clerkenwell. The idea that the government could simply forbid people to meet for the purpose of urging an extension of the franchise was once again to be tested.

What became known as the 'Hyde Park Railings Affair' has been described as the last great action of the London mob. What is certain is that quite apart from the columns of demonstrators heading towards Hyde Park on the evening of 23 July 1866, many ordinary Londoners gathered there because they were angry at this attempt to close off what they believed to be their own space. For working people, living in cramped and crowded conditions, the parks of London were the only green spaces available to them and they resented being told that the police could turn them out at will. They had grown used to being chivvied around by the police and discouraged from treating the streets as their living space; now they were to be forbidden the use of a public park as well.

Sir Richard Mayne himself supervised the barricading of Hyde Park by hundreds of police officers. He had, however, greatly underestimated the strength of opposition to this move, which entailed throwing everybody out of Hyde Park at 5.00 pm on a summer's evening and locking the gates to prevent anybody entering. A journalist from *The Observer* thought that the crowds gathered around Marble Arch and Park Lane numbered hundreds of thousands. It was noticed that these were ordinary families, ranging in age from babes in arms to old men and women. These people were not here as part of a political protest, they simply wished to assert their right to use the park whenever they wanted.

When the crowds outside the park were supplemented by the lines of protesters at Marble Arch, it became clear that the police would not be able to prevent access to Hyde Park. Rather than trying to storm the gates, which were guarded by police constables with truncheons in their hands, attention was given to the railings which enclosed the park. They were weak in places and it did not take long for groups of people to begin rocking them back and forth; loosening and, in the end, tearing them up entirely. Once this was done, the thousands of people crammed into the streets around Marble Arch surged forward, ignoring the police and sweeping into the park. Some of the police officers tried to intervene and were stoned for their troubles.

At this point, the police had little option but to give up the unequal struggle and acknowledge that they had neither the authority nor the physical power to stop Londoners entering what everybody thought of as a public space. Instead, Sir Richard Mayne took the decision to call for military assistance. It was true that the police were being jeered at and their instructions disregarded, but nobody could possibly describe the occupation of the park by countless families, many of them with their children, as a riot. As it was, the arrival of a company of the Grenadier Guards was welcomed enthusiastically by those in the park. The marching soldiers were cheered as they approached and the crowds parted to allow them into Hyde Park. There were cries of, 'Three cheers for the Guards, the people's Guards.' The troops made no attempt to interfere with the civilians, but took up a position near Marble Arch.

Instead of clearing the park at bayonet point, as the police had no doubt expected them to do, the Guards commenced to practice various drill manoeuvres; behaving as though they were on the parade ground and completely ignoring both police and civilians. As the evening drew on, various other army units appeared, including squadrons of cavalry and another company of infantry. It was remarked by all journalists present that the attitude of the crowd towards the soldiers was very warm; a sharp contrast to the way in which they demonstrated what they thought of the police who had done their best to keep them out of Hyde Park. It was midnight when everybody finally left the park; doing so when they were good and ready and showing that the police had in no way at all hurried their departure.

The following day, people began to congregate in the park from very early in the morning. Their aim was to claim Hyde Park as belonging to them, the ordinary men and women of London, rather than to the police or nobility. Riders on Rotten Row were greeted with shouts of, 'What do you want in the people's park?' At dusk, the police sent once more for the army. Again, the soldiers were greeted cheerfully, even when they formed a line and began moving people towards the exits. There were shouts of, 'The Guards, the Guards!' Three squadrons of cavalry helped the Guards to clear the park. A reporter from *The Manchester Guardian* heard some women express the fear that they might be trampled down by the soldiers' horses, but a man near to them was reassuring. He said, 'Never mind the soldiers. They will clear the road, but they won't do you any harm. You're safer with them than those swine of policemen.'

After they had cleared the park, the soldiers were allowed to stand easy and they milled about smoking their pipes and chatting to civilians; making it very clear that they were disgusted to be used in this way against their fellow citizens. When they were finally marched back to the barracks, passers by cheered them on their way.

Throughout the nineteenth-century, soldiers were called into action during riots and industrial disputes, but as police forces grew stronger and acquired more experience of crowd control, it was an increasingly infrequent occurrence. There were very few situations which a properly trained and well-equipped body of police was not able to handle effectively. The answer to civil disorder was found to be making sure there were enough police officers on the ground. It was when this simple concept was neglected that troops were called in, and the results could be disastrous. This was certainly the case in West Yorkshire, during a series of miners' strikes there in 1893.

In late July and early August, 1893, 250,000 miners across Britain went on strike for what they called 'a living wage'. In West Yorkshire, feelings were running exceedingly high. There was the usual anger at what are today called 'blacklegs', but were at that time known by the wonderfully insulting name of 'knobsticks'. At Dewsbury, such strike-breakers had to be escorted to the colliery by police. That a well-organized police force was able to tackle any sort of disorder, if only there were enough of them, was seen very clearly at Dewsbury on 31 July. A mob of over 4,000 striking miners attacked the 'knobsticks' and their police escort. Several lively baton charges by the police were enough to put a stop to the violence.

The effective way that the police had put down disorder in Dewsbury gave the Chief Constable of Yorkshire a false sense of security. Not only did he go off to Scotland on his holidays at the end of August, he even agreed to send 259 officers, a quarter of the entire police force of the West Riding of Yorkshire, to Doncaster on 4 September, to maintain order at the races held there.

The police can cope with rioting and angry crowds, but only if there are enough of them and they are properly directed. With the Chief Constable away and a quarter of the force deployed elsewhere, it was, in retrospect, not surprising that the policing of the miners' strike should run into difficulties. On 5 September, rioting broke out in Barnsley; two collieries were attacked and buildings wrecked by the strikers. The Deputy Chief Constable held a meeting with the local magistrates, as a result of which he contacted the general commanding the army's Northern Division in York and requested military assistance to restore order.

At the town of Featherstone, which lies between Wakefield and Pontefract, was the Ackman Hall Colliery. The miners were on strike, but the surface workers refused to join the strike; a situation which created bitterness among the strikers. There was certainly disorder, with strikers smashing windows and jostling those on their way to work. It was, however, nothing that a large contingent of police could not have handled. Calling in troops was the idea not of the Deputy Chief Constable, but rather the magistrates of Barnsley. It was later suggested that the mine owners had urged this move upon the magistrates, less to preserve order than for the purposes of crushing the strike.

The first group of soldiers arrived at Featherstone station on the evening of Thursday, 7 September. This unit consisted of twenty-nine men of the 1st Battalion South Staffordshire Regiment, commanded by Captain Barker. Nobody appeared to have any clear idea of how the soldiers should be used. They were first marched from the railway station to the colliery; some stones were thrown and there was without doubt a lot of jeering, but no sign of serious disorder.

Once they reached the Ackman Hall Colliery, the soldiers were asked to wait in the engine house; a three-story building. The sight of troops entering their workplace infuriated the strikers and they besieged the engine house, causing Captain Barker and his men to retreat to the third floor. It is possible that some attempt was made to start a fire on the stairs leading to the upper floors of the engine house and when a deal was struck, whereby the strikers agreed to disperse if the soldiers left the premises, then the officer in charge must have breathed a sigh of relief. The men of the South Staffordshire Regiment retreated in good order and it was only when they were back at Featherstone Station that they were able to see that, as soon as they had left, buildings and wagons had been set alight. It was, by now, evening and the flames and smoke could be seen above the rooftops.

Having marched all the way to the colliery and back again, Captain Barker could not have been very pleased when a local magistrate, Bernard Hartley JP, arrived and requested the troops to return to Ackman Hall, where things had now grown considerably more serious. So serious, in fact, that Hartley took the grave step of reading the Riot Act to the crowds. This was at about 8.30 pm. By now, people had come flocking from all across Featherstone and the surrounding area, drawn by the sight of the fires, which were raging in and around the colliery. And still, stones were thrown at the soldiers and also the magistrate, as he stood there ordering them to disperse on pain of being arrested.

It was at this point that the great problem with using troops to suppress moderate disorder was shockingly revealed. There was no suggestion that anybody's life was in danger. True, some empty buildings had been set on fire and stones were being thrown, but it was nothing that a large and determined body of police could not put a stop to by drawing their truncheons and charging. There were, however, no police available; only soldiers who had been trained specifically to kill their enemies as swiftly and effectively as possible.

At 9.15 pm, with less than an hour elapsed since the reading of the Riot Act, Hartley gave a written order to Captain Barker, authorizing him to open fire. However, the magistrate was anxious to avoid loss of life and asked that only blank cartridges be fired. The officer in charge of the troops told Hartley that in the first place, his men were not equipped with blanks and secondly, it was against standing regulations to use blanks under these circumstances. In that case, suggested the magistrate, perhaps Captain Barker's men could fire as little as possible!

The military force present that day at Ackman Hall Colliery faced an almost impossible dilemma. On one hand, they were being called upon by the civil power to use firearms to put down a riot, and on the other, they were asked not to hurt anybody if it could be helped. The officer decided that, initially, he would order only two men to fire at the crowd and to aim at the ground which lay between the soldiers and the mob. Not surprisingly, after the two soldiers had fired and nobody had been hurt, the cry went up from the strikers that the army were only firing blanks. There was much jeering and a new volley of stones, some of which hit the soldiers. At this point, Captain Barker gave the order for a file of eight men to form up; four kneeling and four standing behind them. Then he told them to fire one round into the men surrounding them.

Two men were killed by the shots fired that evening. One was 22-year-old James Gibbs and the other 25-year-old James Arthur Duggan.

Another seven or eight men were wounded. An hour and a half later, reinforcements arrived; men from the Yorkshire Light Infantry and the York and Lancaster Regiment. The shooting had had the desired effect, though, and the town of Featherstone was quiet.

What later came to be known as the Featherstone Massacre was the last time in nineteenth-century Britain when troops opened fire on civilians. It was, by the 1890s, quite plain that dealing with restless crowds with the use of deadly force was not only morally indefensible, it was also likely to backfire on those responsible for initiating the shooting.

Violent crimes such as police murders, mugging and rioting may have been commonplace in nineteenth-century Britain but there was another, more surprising type of criminal activity going on in the heart of Victorian London; the deliberate detonation of a huge quantity of explosives by political extremists, with all the consequent loss of life and damage to property.

Chapter 5

The Clerkenwell Outrage:
Victorian London's 9/11

The worst loss of life in a terrorist attack on the capital took place on 7 July 2005, when fifty-two innocent people, together with the four Islamist bombers, lost their lives in a series of explosions on London's transport system. Most people would perhaps guess that the greatest loss of life in a terrorist bombing in London before this might have taken place during the IRA campaigns of the 1970s and 1980s. In fact, the greatest number of casualties in a terrorist explosion in London before 2005 occurred during the so-called Clerkenwell Outrage almost 140 years earlier; fifteen people died and 120 were injured during this incident. The Clerkenwell Outrage, which entailed the detonation of a quarter of a ton of explosives in a London street, was preceded by, and inextricably linked with, a series of events which took place in the north of England in 1867, which involved the shooting dead of a police officer during an attack by an angry mob.

Between 1866 and 1870, several forays were launched against Canada by Irish nationalists living mainly in the United States. These men represented a relatively new type of Irish nationalism and called themselves Fenians, a general term which encompasses various specific groups; chief of which was the Irish Republican Brotherhood or IRB. In America, a similar organization emerged among Irish emigrees, known as the Fenian Brotherhood. Both were referred to as 'Fenians'. At the same time in the United Kingdom, plans were made for a general rising against British rule in Ireland itself. It would be pointless for bands of men armed only with pikes, shotguns and pitchforks to attack British Army units equipped with the latest repeating rifles so to have any chance of success, such a rebellion would need large quantities of arms. A plan was hatched to seize weapons from the enemy itself. At Chester Castle, in Northern England, there was an arsenal containing 10,000 rifles and over a million rounds of ammunition. This weaponry was guarded by a mere sixty regular soldiers. The group planning the Irish revolt were the Irish Republican Brotherhood, who hoped to overthrow British rule in Ireland and establish a republic there. They decided upon a two-stage attack on Chester Castle and the commandeering of its arms. First, expatriate Irishmen living in Manchester and Liverpool would travel to Chester by train. Once there, they would mount an assault on a smaller arsenal held by the Chester Volunteers; a part-time militia, rather like the modern-day territorial army. Once the crowd was armed with these rifles, the main attack would begin on the castle itself. Trains would be hijacked to carry the stolen weapons to the port of Holyhead in North Wales; from where ships would be seized at gunpoint and used to transport the fighters and their guns across to Ireland.

Although the attempted capture of Chester Castle was a hare-brained scheme with little chance of success, no country can treat lightly a plan to start what is, in effect, an armed uprising on its own soil. Having caught wind of the expedition to Chester, the police ensured that the trains containing the men working for the Irish Republican Brotherhood were shunted into sidings and that other trains with massive army reinforcements were rushed to the city to reinforce those guarding the arsenal. A number of arrests were made, but the ringleaders managed to evade capture. Among them were Colonel Thomas J. Kelly and Captain Timothy Deasy; both of whom had fought for the Confederates during the American Civil War.

In the early hours of 11 September 1867, about six months after the abortive attempt on Chester Castle, two men were arrested in

Manchester on suspicion of attempted robbery. There was a furious struggle when the police laid hold of the men, and both tried to draw revolvers. Up to this moment, there was no reason to suppose that these were anything other than run-of-the-mill petty criminals. One of the men had a strong American accent, both subsequently proved to be Irish-Americans, and it didn't take long to establish that the two men were both wanted in connection with the Chester Castle affair. They were remanded in custody and appeared in court a week later, charged under the Vagrancy Act. This was a holding charge, giving the police more time to gather evidence about the activities of the men. Kelly and Deasy were being escorted from the magistrates court to the police van, which would take them to Manchester's Bellvue prison, when there was a scuffle in the crowd, during which somebody tried to stab a police officer.

After what the police believed to have been a bid to free the Irish prisoners, they decided to take no chances. The two men were manacled and an escort of seven police officers were ordered to accompany the van to the prison. They rode on the roof, while Sergeant Charles Brett was stationed inside the van, with the prisoners.

The van, containing not just the two Irishmen, but also an assortment of ordinary prisoners being remanded for various offences, passed without incident along Hythe Road, which led to the gaol. When it reached the railway viaduct, which passed over the main road, a carefully staged ambush took place. Forty or fifty men, presumably members of the Irish Republican Brotherhood and their sympathizers, were waiting on the other side of the bridge. Some were armed with crowbars and pickaxes, but others were carrying firearms.

The police were only aware of trouble when a volley of shots were fired at them from the crowd that had suddenly materialized around the van. The two horses pulling the van were killed at once, making it impossible to proceed further. The officers on the roof of the van were equipped with cutlasses, but these would not be very helpful when facing a band of gunmen. Nevertheless, they jumped down and did their best to fight back the attackers. One policeman, a detective called Bromley, was shot in the thigh and another was wounded in the back. Seeing that they were so hopelessly outnumbered, the seven men retreated and the crowd then swarmed over the prison van in an attempt to break in to free Kelly and Deasy. This did not prove as easy as they first thought, so somebody tried to shoot out the lock of the door. Unfortunately, at this very moment the police officer in the van, Charles Brett, chose to peer through the keyhole to see what was going on. He fell back with a bullet though his head, which killed him instantly.

Once Sergeant Brett was dead, the prisoners in the van took his keys and opened the door from within. In no time at all, the crowd had dispersed, taking Thomas Kelly and Timothy Deasy with them. Neither of the two men were ever recaptured and it was conjectured that they were later spirited away to America.

The Times published a leader on the day following this incident which could, with minor alterations, have been written the day after the 7/7 bombings on the London Underground. On Thursday, 19 September 1867, it read:

> *It is startling to find ourselves face to face with an armed enemy in one of the most important cities in the kingdom. The Fenians have declared war against our institutions, and have carried it into the very heart of the country.*

Substitute 'Al Qaeda' for 'The Fenians' and one readily imagine these sentences appearing in tomorrow's paper after some terrorist attack.

Despite enormous efforts on the part of the authorities, Kelly and Deasy remained at liberty. Finding members of the mob which had launched the assault on the prison van was easier, some of them were seized almost immediately after attack. Within a week, the police had arrested a total of twenty-eight men and charged them with the murder of Sergeant Brett. Of course, only one man had fired the shot which actually killed the unfortunate officer, but in law all those who had been part of the joint enterprise were equally guilty. Readers will perhaps recognize that the affair at Manchester fell into the category of a 'freedom riot', where a crowd of people set out with the aim of releasing prisoners from police custody by the use of force.

On 28 September 1867, the twenty-eight men who had been arrested for the attack on the prison van and murder of Sergeant Brett appeared at a magistrates court in Manchester. Two were discharged; leaving twenty-six to be remanded in custody to face trial for murder. Nobody was taking any further chances with security and troops had been drafted in to escort the accused men to and from the court. Even the most ruthless and determined Fenian would hesitate to launch an attack against the squadron of dragoons who rode alongside the prison vans.

It was clear to the authorities that the conviction and hanging of twenty-six men for the death of one police officer would look vengeful and provide a propaganda victory for the Irish nationalists. When the trial opened on 28 October 1867, only five men entered the dock; the remaining twenty-one had been discharged. All five were convicted of murder and sentenced to death. There was reason to think that one of the defendants, William Phillip Allen, had actually fired the shot which killed Sergeant Brett. As for the other four men, it was enough to prove that they had been part of the mob, which had set out to free the two men in the prison van.

All of the five men tried for Sergeant Brett's murder were convicted. One of the men was pardoned and freed almost immediately. This was Thomas Maguire, who had been serving with the Royal Marines for ten years. It had been his misfortune both to have found himself quite by chance in the vicinity of the attack on the van and to be obviously Irish. He was pardoned and allowed to rejoin his regiment. Another of those condemned to death, O'Meagher Condon, was an American citizen. Unwilling to provoke a dispute with the United States, this man's sentence was commuted to penal servitude for life. The remaining three men, William Philip Allen, Michael Larkin and Michael O'Brien, would all hang for their part in Sergeant Brett's murder.

The executions took place publicly on Saturday, 23 November 1867; all three men were hanged side by side on the same scaffold. Nobody was disposed to take any chances of a last-minute attempt at rescue and in addition to the regular police on duty that day, 2,500 special constables had also been sworn in. The gallows upon which the men were to hang had been erected against the wall of the prison and it was thought that if any efforts to free the condemned men were undertaken, it would be when they were brought out of the prison and led up onto the scaffold. Troops were accordingly quartered in the prison; a detachment of Highlanders, along with a company of artillery. Before the execution began, troops with fixed bayonets surrounded the scaffold, as well as taking position on a nearby railway viaduct.

The hangings proceeded as a smoothly as could have been wished and were witnessed by a crowds of perhaps 10,000 people on a foggy and overcast morning. There were two minor incidents, the first of which was that Larkin fainted before the drop fell. He was supported by two prison warders, who sprang off the trap at the last moment. More alarmingly, almost as soon as the three men were launched into eternity, there came the sound of two sharp explosions. The soldiers guarding the scaffold, cocked their weapons and began looking around for targets, but the bangs were caused only by fog warnings on the nearby railway line.

With the execution of the murderers of Sergeant Brett and the flight of those supposedly responsible for the plan to attack Chester Castle, the authorities began to relax; it looked as though the worst of the danger was over. In fact, the events in Manchester were only the curtain-raiser for a far greater tragedy, which was to be enacted in London less than a month later.

The police strongly suspected that the attack on the prison van, which had led to the murder of Sergeant Brett, had been organized by another Irishman who had spent a lot of time in the USA. Ricard O'Sullivan Burke was twenty-nine years of age and had travelled the world extensively. He had fought in the American Civil War and held a commission in the Union Army; unusually for a Fenian, most of whom were on the side of the Confederates. O'Sullivan-Burke had worked with Thomas Kelly, one of those freed in the raid on the prison van, and that year he had procured a quantity of arms and attempted to smuggle them into Ireland.

Following the freeing of Kelly and Deasy, the police throughout Britain were on the lookout for Ricard O'Sullivan Burke. Three days before the executions in Manchester, Inspector James Thompson of the Metropolitan Police was patrolling the Bloomsbury district of central London. He turned a corner into Woburn Square and quite literally bumped into the most wanted man in the country. Ricard O'Sullivan Burke was not alone. He was in the company of another member of the Irish Republican Brotherhood, a man called Joseph Casey. Inspector Thompson arrested both of them and took the two men to the nearby police station in Holborn.

There was, not unnaturally, considerable anxiety on the part of the authorities about the possibility of a rescue attempt being made on the two senior Fenians being held at Holborn police station. As soon as they had been charged, O'Sullivan Burke with treason-felony and Casey with assaulting a police officer, the two of them were at once transferred on remand to the Clerkenwell House of Detention; a forbidding and all but impregnable prison, just to the east of Farringdon Road.

By early December, 1867, the government were congratulating themselves on having dealt very neatly with the crisis caused by resurgent, militant Irish nationalism. The rising in Ireland had been foiled, the incursions from America into Canada repulsed and the death of the Manchester police officer avenged. It was felt that matters had been handled with great skill and that, with luck, it would be some years before the next trouble erupted over the question of home rule for Ireland. In fact, the worst was yet to come.

The Clerkenwell House of Detention was an exceedingly secure Victorian gaol. It was surrounded by a 25-foot high wall. A surviving section of this wall may be seen in Plate 9. Prisoners were kept locked in their cells for most of the day, except for an hour's exercise each afternoon. The exercise yard was behind that enormous wall. Surely it would be impossible for anybody to breach that wall and rescue the men?

In the first week of December, rumours reached the police that O'Sullivan Burke and Casey were to be rescued from prison. The information was quite specific: the external wall of the gaol would be 'mined'. You might think that after the attack in Manchester, such a warning would be treated with the utmost seriousness and some extra precautions were certainly taken. Armed guards were posted on the prison roof, in order to shoot anybody trying to enter or leave the place under suspicious circumstances. Extra police were detailed to patrol the streets surrounding the Clerkenwell House of Detention.

It was known in the prison that a group of Fenians had rented a room in nearby Woodbridge Street; a room with a window which overlooked the exercise yard of the prison. It might be thought that, with everybody on high alert, anything a bit out of the ordinary would be spotted and investigated; all of which makes the events of Thursday, 12 December 1867 all the more shocking. Yet we have the memoirs of the former Assistant Commissioner of Police, Sir Robert Anderson, as well as many witnesses, such as police officers and warders at the prison. The subsequent events were sifted through exhaustively and there can be little doubt about the sequence of truly astonishing blunders, which occurred both that day and the next.

At 3.30 pm, while the prisoners were walking silently round the exercise yard, a man with a handcart entered Corporation Row, the narrow street which lay alongside the exercise yard, and unloaded a large barrel, which he placed against the wall of the prison. He then produced a small, white, India-rubber ball, which he lobbed over the wall and into the area where the prisoners were exercising. As soon as O'Sullivan Burke and Casey saw this ball, they both pretended to have stones in their shoes and dropped out of the line of men patiently plodding round the courtyard. They went over to a corner, crouched down and began fiddling with their shoes. A warder who spotted the thrown ball picked it up and put it into his pocket to take home for his son. It did not occur to him that there might have been anything out of the ordinary about somebody tossing a ball over the high perimeter wall.

If the warder supervising the exercise yard showed a lamentable lack of curiosity, it is almost impossible to find words adequately to describe the conduct of the police officer who was standing guard in Corporation Row, supposedly on the watch for suspicious activity. He had watched with bovine incuriosity as the huge barrel had been placed against the wall of the gaol and remained watching as the man who had placed it there put a fuse in the side, lit it and then dashed for cover. The fuse went out and the man who had lit it returned and tried again; once more running frantically from the scene after applying a match to the fuse. Again, it went out and was by this time so short, that the man in charge of the barrel evidently did not feel inclined to risk another attempt. Instead, he rolled the barrel back onto the handcart and trundled out of sight.

Later that day, the constable who had witnessed the performance with the barrel reported the matter to his sergeant, and it was only then that it began to dawn on the police that a rescue attempt had actually been carried out before their very eyes.

It might have been thought that after making such a mess of things on the Thursday, the police would have tightened up their security the following day. They knew that an escape attempt was planned and had failed the previous day; surely they might have assumed that this would not be the end of the matter?

Friday, 13 December dawned; a chilly, grey day which remained overcast from morning to dusk. The warders, unlike the police, were apparently taking the threat of some sort of assault on the prison with the gravity it deserved. Every day, cooked meals had been delivered to the prison for the two Fenians being held on remand. These were brought to the prison by an Englishwoman called Anne Justice. This woman had been seen talking to the Irishmen who had rented the room overlooking the prison yard. At 3.00 pm, a warder spotted her talking to a rough-looking man on the corner of Corporation Row. They seemed to him to be behaving in a furtive manner and he fetched another guard to see what he made of it. With all the talk of escape, the staff at the Clerkenwell House of Detention were on edge and not minded to take any chances. Half an hour later, Anne Justice was seen again; this time in an upper-story room of a house in Woodbridge Street. Two warders could see a group of men in the room with her and they were all staring anxiously towards Corporation Row.

In Corporation Row itself, PC Moriarty was on duty. He had been warned to be on the alert for anybody trying to break into the prison by means of a 'mine'. Like other police officers, Moriarty took this to mean that people might try to dig beneath the walls and tunnel into the gaol. Of course, to 'mine' a structure can have quite a different meaning; as PC Moriarty was soon to discover.

It was growing dark when a horse and cart stopped at the junction of Corporation Row and Woodbridge Street. Two men rolled a barrel down and manoeuvred it into position against the wall. It almost defies belief, but PC Moriarty remained where he was, watching this as though it had nothing to do with him. The horse and cart left, leaving one of the two men to produce two fireworks. He approached a group of boys standing and smoking. He gave one of the fireworks to them and begged a light from them; he lit one of the squibs, went back to the barrel and poked it in a hole and ran for his life. And still, PC Moriarty stood, observing the entire episode.

Experiments later carried out showed that a barrel of the size used by the men that day would hold exactly 548 pounds of fine grain gunpowder. This amounts to a little over a quarter of a ton; a truly awesome quantity of explosives. Corporation Row was a narrow, residential street. The high prison wall faced a line of terraced houses occupied in the main by manual workers. Because it was a working day, most of the men were away and the houses contained only women and children.

The explosion that afternoon was heard across the whole of London and there were reports that it had been audible 20 miles away. Witnesses who were some miles from Clerkenwell described the sound as being like the discharge of artillery. Sixty feet of the prison's perimeter wall disintegrated. The houses on the other side of the street were destroyed; those which remained standing were so badly damaged that they had to be demolished a few days later. Windows were shattered and chimney pots brought down a mile from the site of the explosion. The sheer force of the barrel of gunpowder may be more readily appreciated if we look at a section of the perimeter wall of the Clerkenwell House of Detention which is still standing. Plate 9 shows this part of the wall today. That a 60-foot long section of this wall could be reduced to rubble is testament to the immense power of the explosion.

The blast from a large explosion of this kind is unpredictable. Sometimes, those nearby are left almost untouched, while another person some distance away is killed outright. So it was with the Clerkenwell explosion. PC Moriarty was only 20 or 30 yards from the barrel when it was detonated and yet he was unscathed. The only injury he suffered was to his dignity; the force of the blast knocked him to the ground and also ripped his clothes off. When he got to his feet, it was to find that he was completely naked!

As the echoes of the explosion died away, people came running to the scene to see if they could help. The warders inside the prison, mistaking them for Fenian attackers, began firing at them.

Luckily for O'Sullivan Burke and Casey, they had not been in the exercise yard when the barrel of gunpowder went off. Because of all the rumours, the governor had arranged for the men to walk round the yard in the morning, rather than the afternoon. Had he not done so, then the death toll would have been even greater than it was. The debris from the shattered wall had scythed across the yard; smashing into the main prison building. Anybody who had been standing in that area would at the very least have been gravely injured and more likely killed.

By the time that any rescue work could be organized to search for survivors in the rubble of the houses on Corporation Row, it was quite dark. Troops had been sent to guard the prison and the police worked grimly, sifting through the heaps of plaster and broken bricks. Six bodies were unearthed more or less at once. These included a 65-year-old woman called Martha Evans and a 7-year-old child called Minnie Abbot. Another nine casualties died in hospital. Over forty people were seriously injured by the blast, to the extent that they lost limbs or were blinded, and another eighty received minor cuts and bruises. The human cost was not limited to physical injuries. The row of houses facing the prison wall was almost completely demolished, but 400 other houses were also damaged. A total of 600 families suffered loss of housing, damage to furniture and other harm to property.

The panic that followed the attack on the House of Detention was remarkable. Rumours circulated that the bombing was to be the signal for Irishmen living in London to rise up and launch a war against the government. Troops were mobilized and 20,000 special constables enrolled to guard everywhere from arsenals and gasworks, to the British Museum. Almost immediately, demands were made for emergency powers and, most ominously, the suspension of *Habeus Corpus*. The feverish atmosphere was very similar, in many ways, to that which followed the 9/11 attacks in the United States.

Some idea of the hysteria which gripped even those at the heart of government may be gauged from looking at the letters written over the next few days by the then Chancellor of the Exchequer, Benjamin Disraeli. With Lord Derby, the Prime Minister, out of London, Disraeli felt that responsibility for meeting what he saw as a grave crisis devolved upon him. The day after the Clerkenwell Outrage, Disraeli wrote to the Prime Minister, telling him that, 'affairs here are very serious'. He went on;

> *There is no doubt that there is a system of organised incendiarism afloat, and we credibly hear of men coming from America, who are to take empty houses in various parts of London, and set them on fire, probably simultaneously.*

Having raised the spectre of a second Great Fire of London, Disraeli went on to propose draconian measures for dealing with the supposed threat. His letter continued, 'Many of the miscreants who are to perpetrate these crimes are now here, and are known – and we can't touch them. I think *Habeus Corpus* ought to be suspended.'

It is quite impossible, 150 years later, to know whether or not Disraeli, who was soon to become Prime Minister himself, really believed what he was telling Lord Derby, or if he was exaggerating the threat in order to acquire special powers. He said in another letter that a plot had been uncovered, which involved gunpowder being introduced into the Houses of Parliament via the gas pipes; so enabling terrorists to blow the place up. In another letter to the Prime Minister on 17 December, he claimed to have received information that a band of thirty Fenians had set sail from America who had sworn a solemn oath to assassinate the queen and every member of the cabinet. Disraeli's suggested course of action was to send the Royal Navy to intercept the ship in international waters, board it and remove the men. There was, as Disraeli himself freely admitted, a slight drawback to this plan, which was that stopping a ship on the high seas in this way was tantamount to an act of war. As he admitted in another letter to Lord Derby, 'If stopped on the high seas, we may be involved in a war with America.'

Whether Disraeli was making a play for power or perhaps genuinely did not appreciate the risks that he was running, his actions were dangerous and we may, in retrospect, be grateful that he was granted neither the emergency powers he wished for, nor permission to start a war with the United States. When all was said and done, the terrible explosion in Clerkenwell was not the opening shot in an attempt to destroy London or overthrow the government; it was simply a tragic miscalculation. Those who had set off the barrel of gunpowder had no idea how much damage a quarter of a ton of explosives would cause in a built up area.

It was not hard for the police to round up the Irishmen who had rented the room overlooking the prison yard. Anne Justice was arrested at the same time and she tried to hang herself that very night. Over the next few days, both Justice and the two Irishmen who had been living in the room which had been used as an observation post, began trying to save themselves from the shadow of the gallows by informing on the man who had carried out the attack. It appeared that a Fenian called Michael Barrett had arrived in London from Glasgow and that the whole operation had been his work. He had acquired the explosives and detonated them. Those being held on the charge of murder gave sufficient information to enable the police to find Barrett in Glasgow, so that he could be brought back to London and put on trial with the others.

Meanwhile, it was left to the Home Secretary and the Commissioner of Police for the Metropolis to explain how it was possible for the bombing in Clerkenwell to have been carried out literally under the eyes of the police. They had, after all, been specifically warned by an informer that an attempt was to be made to demolish, by means of a mine, the wall surrounding the Clerkenwell House of Detention. The explanation for this piece of ineptitude offered to the House of Commons by Home Secretary Gathorne Hardy was stunning. It appeared that confusion had been caused by the fact that the information received by the police suggested that the prison wall was to be blown *up*, whereas it had in fact been blown *down*. To understand how this fine, semantic difference might have put the police off their guard, we cannot do better than to quote from the statement made by the Home Secretary;

> *It appeared that the mode of carrying out the design of which they had received information did not strike those who were set to watch the outside of the prison … What their attention was apparently directed to was the undermining of the wall; they thought it would probably be blown up from underneath, and had no conception that it would be blown down in the way it really was done.*

Little wonder that the Commissioner of Police felt obliged to tender his resignation, which was inexplicably refused.

In the spring of 1868, the trial took place of the four men and one woman who were charged with the murders of those who had died in the explosion. The trial and aftermath are notable for leading to one of the last manifestations of a particular type of London mob; the crowd surrounding the scaffold at a public hanging.

Anne Justice, whose only real offence had been hanging round with a bunch of Fenian sympathizers, was the first to be dealt with. The jury did not even wait to hear the defence case before acquitting her. The four men remained in the dock. Two of these, Timothy Desmond and Jeremiah Allen, were the men who had rented the room near the Clerkenwell House of Detention. Also accused was Michael Barrett, the man from Glasgow and also a man called James O'Neill; whose chief offence seemed to be that he had rented Barrett a room. He too was swiftly acquitted of murder. Desmond and Allen then struck a deal with the prosecutor, whereby they were granted immunity in exchange for giving evidence against Michael Barrett. Their evidence was that the whole plot had been Barrett's doing and that they had known nothing of what was being planned.

In the end, Michael Barrett alone stood in the dock at the Old Bailey, facing trial for the worst terrorist attack that had ever been seen in this country. The evidence was clear enough and he was convicted and sentenced to death. In addition to the infamy of having probably caused more injuries and loss of life by one single act than anybody in British history, Barrett went on to achieve fame for another footnote in British judicial history.

Before the establishment of official police forces, the staging of regular, public, mass executions was the only real deterent to potential criminals; from murderers down topickpockets and vandals. There were two chief objections to this method of tackling crime. The first being that it was, quite simply, ineffective. Savage punishments are less effective in discouraging people from committing crimes than the probability of being caught. However terrible the penalty, if the odds are a million to one against suffering it, then more people are likely to take the risk. If, on the other hand, there is an excellent chance of being arrested and brought to court, potential offenders tend to think twice; even if the punishment faced is only a year or two's imprisonment.

That public hangings were pointless as far as deterring or even affecting criminal behaviour was one objection to their continued existence. The other was that the awful spectacle which they provided was hardly suitable for a modern, civilized society, which was trying to impose new standards of decency and good behaviour in public. The crowds who gathered to witness hangings showed the London mob at its very worst. In Georgian London, hanging days had been like carnivals, with apprentices traditionally granted the day off to go and attend executions. The Industrial Revolution and the dawning of the Enlightenment had done nothing to diminish the appetite for public executions. The crowds attending such events were enormous; 20,000 or more being not uncommon. In 1864, at the hanging of the five so-called *Flowery Land* pirates outside Newgate Prison, it was estimated that 200,000 people were present. The new technology of Victorian Britain was harnessed to make these exhibitions more easily accessible. Special excursion trains were laid on to towns where a hanging was to take place. Far from acting as a warning to criminals, the vast numbers of spectators proved an irresistible draw to pickpockets and muggers. In the late eighteenth-century, when picking pockets was a capital crime, hanging days were one of the most profitable locations for this offence; its practitioners working both literally and metaphorically in the shadow of the gallows.

It was generally accepted that public executions revealed the 'mob' at its worst. Writing to *The Times* on 13 November 1849, Charles Dickens provides a graphic description of the behaviour of the mob at a hanging that year in London; the execution of the Mannings at Horsemonger Lane prison.

I was a witness at the execution at Horsemonger Lane this morning. I went there with the intention of observing the crowd to behold it, and I had excellent opportunities of doing so, at intervals all through the night, and continuously from day-break until after the spectacle was over. I believe that a sight so inconceivably awful as the wickedness and levity of the immense crowd collected at that execution this morning could be imagined by no man, and could be presented in no heathen land under the sun. The horrors of the gibbet and of the crime which brought the wretched murders to it faded in my mind before the atrocious bearing, looks and language of the assembled spectators. When I came upon the scene at midnight, the shrillness of the cries

The Gordon Riots of 1780; hundreds die as the army restores order in London.

The Calthorpe Arms, where PC Robert Culley died, following a riot in 1833.

The frame used to secure garrotters while they were being flogged.

A modern mosaic commemorating the Newport Rising of 1839. More than twenty people died.

CHARTISTS' RIOTS.

Police officers seek to put down a Chartist inspired riot in 1839.

A garrotter, after he has been flogged in 1864.

Garrotters at work, mugging a well-to-do victim.

Rioting in Hyde Park in 1866. The Grenadier Guards have been called out.

A surviving part of the wall of Clerkenwell Prison. In 1867, a 60 foot long section was demolished by a quarter of a ton of explosives.

The murder of Sergeant Brett by an angry mob in 1867.

The aftermath of the Clerkenwell Outrage; fifteen people died in the explosion and over a hundred were injured.

PUNCH, OR THE LONDON CHARIVARI—December 28, 1867.

GUNPOWL

THE FENIAN GUY FAWKES.

A cartoon in *Punch* about the Clerkenwell Outrage.

The bomb attack in Parliament Street in 1883.

Scotland Yard after the explosion of 1884.

The damage caused to the Tower of London by a bomb detonated there in 1885.

Rioting in Hyde Park, 1884.

Black Monday, 1886; also known as the West End Riots.

Bloody Sunday in London, 1887. Three men were killed in the rioting.

The 1897 Aldersgate tube bombing.

1897, the first fatality resulting from a terrorist strike against London's underground.

and howls that were raised from time to time, denoting that they came from a concourse of boys and girls already assembled in the best places, made my blood run cold … When the day dawned, thieves, low prostitutes, ruffians and vagabonds of every kind, flocked onto the ground, with every variety of offensive and foul behaviour. Fightings, faintings, whistlings, imitations of Punch, brutal jokes, tumultuous demonstrations of indecent delight when swooning women were dragged out of the crowd by the police, with their dresses disordered, gave a new zest to the general entertainment.

This was the 'mob' at its very worst and as the century drew on, there were increasing demands that such terrible displays were halted; having no place in the modern world. The *Capital Punishment within Prisons Act* was due to receive Royal assent only a few days after the date scheduled for Michael Barrett's execution. By sheer chance, he became the last person to be publicly executed in this country.

Although the breaking down of the railings which surrounded Hyde Park has been called the last action of the 'London mob', the hanging of Michael Barrett for the Clerkenwell Outrage, which took place two years later, might perhaps be another contender for the final appearance of the London mob. The scenes on the night of 25 May, 1868 were pretty much exactly as Dickens had described them twenty years earlier.

Barrett, a 27-year-old labourer, rose at 6.00 am and took communion on the morning of his execution. Two hours later the hangman, William Calcraft, came to his cell to pinion the condemned man and lead him to the gallows, which had been erected outside Newgate; the site where the Central Criminal Court now stands. Calcraft had been the official hangman for over forty years by this time and was an old man with a reputation for bungling. Most of his victims choked to death, rather than dying cleanly by having their necks broken.

When Barrett and the executioner stepped onto the scaffold, there were cheers, followed by hisses and catcalls before the crowd fell silent. Calcraft pulled the white hood over the condemned man's head and adjusted the noose. Barrett turned to him and asked that the noose be loosened a little. This was done and then, with no further delay, the lever was pulled and Britain's last public execution was completed.

The Clerkenwell Outrage is worth examining for several reasons; not least for the last glimpse of the traditional London 'mob'. It is also surprising that it was to be almost 150 years before a terrorist action caused greater loss of life in Britain. Another minor historical note is that, after the execution of Michael Barrett, it became the custom in London to refer to Irishmen as 'Mick Barretts'. In time, the surname was dropped, leaving only the pejorative expression 'Micks', which lingers on to this day.

The Clerkenwell Outrage and the murder of a police officer which precipitated it, tells us a good deal about public order in the late 1860s. The killing of a police officers by a mob was still something that happened from time to time in some parts of the country, although it was definitely on the decline. It is particularly interesting that in the aftermath of the most devastating attack on London for centuries, the first instinct of the government was *not* to call out the army. True, some soldiers were used in the days following the explosion, to guard the prison and patrol parts of central London, for instance, but responsibility for tackling the affair was recognized as being the duty of the police. Many special constables were sworn in, but these were soon discharged, because the regular police proved capable of dealing with the situation. The way to handle such a dreadful crime was not to use the army, but rather to rely upon the police to track down those responsible and bring them before the courts.

Another aspect of British policing which has, for many years, been taken for granted, yet distinguishes British police from those of almost any other country in the world, is the fact that our police have always been unarmed. It is almost an article of faith that the British Bobby on the beat has rarely carried anything more fearsome than a wooden stick.

This is yet another myth. In fact for much of their existence, the British police have regularly been armed.

Chapter 6

The Myth of the Unarmed Police Force: The Police Response to Gun Crime in the 1870s and 1880s

O f all the crimes to bedevil modern British society, the most alarming are probably those involving firearms. In London and other big cities, gun crime is, seemingly, endemic. In response to the increasing use of guns by criminals and also to combat the threat of terrorism, the police too have taken to carrying guns. Thirty years ago, the sight of a British police officer with a gun was all but unheard of; today, we see them at airports and railway stations, guarding the entrance to Downing Street and even on patrol in the streets. This surely is not how things used to be? Until recently, wasn't it the case that police officers were able to tackle crime armed with no more than a wooden truncheon to defend themselves and a whistle to summon aid? Is this an accurate picture, or a powerful and enduring myth?

There never was a time when all police in Britain were unarmed and wholly reliant upon nothing more than a short, wooden stick of the type carried by Mr Punch. Indeed, for some years, the police in London and elsewhere were routinely armed; carrying revolvers every time they went on duty after dark. To see how this situation arose, which, like so much to do with the history of British law and order, has been lost to memory, it will be necessary to go back to the earliest days of the modern police and see what was happening before the establishment of the Metropolitan Police in 1829.

Before a city-wide police force was founded for the capital, there were various local arrangements for law enforcement; the so-called 'Bow Street Runners', for instance. The members of this force, more correctly known as 'principle officers', were armed with either pistols or cutlasses, sometimes with both and also, on occasion, blunderbusses. These weapons were necessary because many of those they encountered were likely to be armed. From 1782, the Bow Street Foot Patrol covered central London and in 1792 was expanded to include areas such as Whitechapel and Southwark. The seven subsidiary offices set up in that year were all stocked with pistols, which were regularly carried by the officers on the streets.

In 1798, another police force was set up to patrol the river Thames. The Thames River Public Office was based in Wapping and its officers were armed with flintlock pistols. London was plagued by robberies in the late eighteenth and early nineteenth centuries; some carried out on foot and others on horseback. The mounted robbers were generally known as highwaymen and those without horses as footpads. Many highway robberies took place on the lonely roads leading into London and so, in 1805, the Bow Street Horse Patrol began. These men operated up to 20 miles from Bow Street and all were armed with pistols and sabres. The alarming increase in the prevalence of street robberies on foot, what we would today call muggings, led in 1821 to the formation of the oddly named Dismounted Horse Patrol, whose members were just ordinary officers who patrolled the streets on foot. Every one of them was armed with a pistol.

Until the formation of the Metropolitan Police in 1829, it seems to have been taken for granted that police officers needed to be equipped with firearms. The idea of unarmed police simply did not appear to have occurred to anybody. Indeed, as late as the beginning of 1829, the Bow Street Day Patrol was described in *A Treatise on the Police and Crimes in the Metropolis*, published in 1829, as being 'well armed'.

Perhaps it was fears that a regular police force could easily develop into a tool of the state for the suppression of liberty that, when the Metropolitan Police began in 1829, it was announced that it was to be an unarmed body. They would, it was suggested, carry nothing more dangerous than short staves. From the beginning though, this assurance was not to be taken at face value.

When the Metropolitan Police was set up, it was run by two commissioners; Lieutenant Colonel Charles Rowan and Richard Mayne. In December 1829, just three months after the first officers appeared on the streets, Richard Mayne ordered the receiver of the new police force, John Wray, who was responsible for finance and equipment, to purchase fifty pairs of flintlock pistols. A hundred pistols, at a time when there were only 1,000 officers in the whole police force, suggests that it was always intended that a certain number of officers would be armed. It took years for the other police forces operating in London, such as the River Public Office and the Bow Street Mounted Patrol, to be incorporated into the Metropolitan Police and even after this happened, these units remained permanently armed. The Bow Street Horse Patrol was absorbed by the Metropolitan Police in 1836, but the officers of this force kept their pistols. The evidence that the mounted police were, during Victoria's reign, an armed force is indirect but compelling. In December 1852, a permanent under-secretary at the Home Office wrote to the receiver for the Metropolitan Police to let him know that Home Secretary Spencer Walpole had approved a contract for new saddles for the mounted police, which would include cartridge boxes; a clear indication that there was no secret about the armed nature of the mounted police at this time.

Following the establishment of the new police force in London, other provincial cities and counties also began setting up regular police forces. Some of these were armed from the beginning. When the city of Nottingham created a police force modelled on that of London, in

1836, one of the first steps was to acquire firearms. These consisted of flintlock pistols engraved with the words, 'Nottingham Police'.

It seems likely that senior officers at this time were always armed, in London at least. A tender for supplying equipment to the Metropolitan Police for the three years ending 31 December 1859 contains some revealing information. That mounted officers routinely carried sabres and pistols is known, but hidden away among the estimated costs of such items as rattles at 5 shillings each and handcuffs at four shillings and sixpence a pair, we find things like powder flasks, sabres and 'Pistols, with Swivel Ramrods, for Inspectors'. There are also estimates for pistols, 'for Mounted Men'. It certainly appears that as late as 1859, the police in London were not really an unarmed force at all.

Not all the pistols used by the police in London were old-fashioned flintlock and percussion lock weapons. In 1854, officers at the Woolwich Dockyard were issued with Colt revolvers. Other forces were also switching to revolvers at this time. The Warwickshire Constabulary were acquiring revolvers and the Warrington Borough Police were, at the same time, issued with enough revolvers for every member of the force.

The Fenian attacks of 1867 in Manchester and London provided the impetus to modernize the firearms used generally by the British police. It was at this time that the first organized training in the use of firearms began for the police in London. A week after the Clerkenwell Outrage, fifty constables, drawn from across the capital, went to the rifle range at Wormwood Scrubs, where they were given systematic instruction in the use of revolvers. A few days later, on Christmas Eve 1867, another fifty constables, together with four inspectors, went down to Wormwood Scrubs for training. On Boxing Day, forty-two men were instructed in pistol shooting at Peckham and the following day, another fifty at Wormwood Scrubs. By the end of December, it appeared that the intention was for every police officer in London to become proficient in the use of firearms; those who had attended these training sessions were given responsibility to go back to their stations and teach all the men there what they had learned.

The following year, over 600 Adams breach loading revolvers were supplied to the Metropolitan Police by the armoury at the Tower of London. Sixty-three sergeants from police stations across the capital were instructed to collect ten weapons each and take them back for the use of their men.

It is plain from this evidence that, despite any public statements to the contrary, various police forces in this country were maintaining stocks of firearms and ensuring that these were readily available and their men knew how to use them. The issuing of firearms became such a regular occurrence that it would no longer be reasonable to describe the police in this country as 'unarmed'.

The use of firearms by criminals on the streets of Britain appears, to many of us, to be a disturbing and relatively new phenomenon. Gangland killings, teenagers shooting each other over trifling disputes about territory, drive-by shootings; these have all become a feature of life in certain parts of our larger cities. Often, such offences are clustered together in small areas; for example Hackney in East London. Lower Clapton Road in that district is known locally as 'Murder Mile', because of the appalling number of shootings which take place there. In a two-year period, no fewer than eight men have been shot dead in and around this otherwise unremarkable street. Other parts of the borough are similarly plagued with gun crime. A recent week saw seven shootings in as many days. In parts of some British cities, gun crime is viewed as just a regrettable part of modern life.

Looking back at the statistics for such crimes in the nineteenth-century and browsing contemporary newspaper reports and court transcripts, we can compare gun crime in modern society with that of Victorian society. The results of such research are quite shocking. Beginning with the number of police officers shot dead in this country between 1993 and 2013; the most recent figures available at the time of writing. There were eight such murders; none of which took place in London. Yet during a similar twenty-year period in the late nineteeth century, from 1875 to 1895, no fewer than seventeen police officers were shot dead. In other words, the rate of police murders by the use of firearms in London was running at roughly twice what it is today.

A quick look at newspaper reports over this same period also reveals something quite surprising. It is popularly supposed that a lot of the gun crime these days takes place in areas where there are a high concentration of people of Afro-Caribbean origin; Hackney, Tottenham and Peckham in London, for example, and parts of Manchester, Birmingham and Nottingham. Popular opinion is not always wrong and in this case is spot on. A Freedom of Information request by a journalist from the *Daily Telegraph*, a few years ago, brought forth the interesting statistic that although only 12 per cent of the population in the capital are black, 67 per cent of those proceeded against for firearms offences were from that group. The picture is similar in other large cities with established Afro-Caribbean communities. This is true, as far as it goes, but it is curious to note that those same areas were where gun crime was most common in the Victorian era, too. Looking now at incidents when police officers were shot at, but not necessarily killed, the area covered by the present day London Borough of Hackney features heavily. Indeed, some of the newspaper reports from the late nineteenth-century could have been taken straight from yesterday's newspapers.

Today, Clapton Road in Hackney is known locally as 'Murder Mile', due to the number of shootings which have taken place in and around the street. Were things more peaceful and orderly in the later years of Victoria's reign?

In the early hours of the morning of 23 January 1882, police constables William Stapleton and William Grover were patrolling Clapton Road when they saw two men leaving a house in nearby Brook

Road. It was three in the morning and so they approached the men and asked what they were up to. For reply, one of the men drew a pistol and pointed it at the officers, telling them, 'Stop, you bastards. Come any closer and I'll shoot you.' Then the two men ran off, with the policemen in pursuit. However, they lost the suspects somewhere near Hackney Downs.

A little over a week later, PC Edward Reany was walking his beat in Dalston, not far from Clapton Road and another district noted today for shootings and general disorder. He heard somebody call out, 'Stop thief!' Two other officers were nearby and Reany saw a man walking towards him, in a slow and apparently unconcerned fashion. He approached this man and said, 'What's up, old man?' Whereupon the man to whom he spoke pulled out a revolver, brandished it at the three constables and asked, 'Which of you will have this?'

PC Reany shouted a warning to the others and then moved towards the gunman, who at once opened fire. Showing incredible bravery, Reany knocked the man down and disarmed him. By enormous good fortune, the bullet had gone through the police officer's coat. The man with the revolver was later identified as Edward Franklin; he was the same person who had threatened PC Stapleton with his gun a week earlier.

It would not be surprising to hear of this kind incident happening in Dalston this week. Even over a century ago, this was par for the course in that corner of Hackney. Later that year, only a few hundred yards from the spot where PC Reany was shot at, there was an even more shocking instance of the casual way in which guns were being used on the streets of London.

On the night of 1 December 1882, Police Constable George Cole, a young and newly married man, had just left Dalston police station for night duty on the streets of Hackney. It was a foggy evening and when he turned into Ashwin Street, a turning off Dalston Lane, he saw a shadowy figure who seemed to him to be trying to break into the

Baptist Chapel. PC Cole arrested the young man and was about to lead him to the police station when a shot rang out. The young officer fell to the ground, mortally wounded. Two women who had witnessed the shooting hurried to the police station to raise the alarm. Because it was so dark and foggy, they were unable to give much of a description of the man who had shot PC Cole, other than that he had been wearing a black hat.

Sergeant Cobb, the officer's immediate superior, was first on the scene, but he was too late to save Cole. Scattered on the pavement were various articles, which had obviously been dropped by the murderer. There was a black, felt 'wideawake' hat and two chisels, which had most likely been used as housebreaking implements. Of the man who had shot the young constable, there was no sign at all.

Then, as now, the police made it their business to keep an eye on young tearaways and hooligans and Sergeant Cobb remembered that he had seen a local youth that very evening who was wearing just such a hat as the one found at the scene of the murder. He put out word that Thomas Henry Orrock was to be brought in for questioning. Orrock, nineteen years of age at the time, came from a respectable family, but was going off the rails. He was soon arrested and took part in an identity parade, but the night had been so dark and foggy that neither of the two women who had witnessed the shooting were able positively to identify him. He was accordingly released.

There was one more clue to the murder, but it was one whose significance was overlooked. On the blade of one of the chisels was scratched the word, 'rock'. In retrospect, it was obvious that this was part of Orrock's name, which he had scratched on the tool to claim ownership.

Over a year passed. Sergeant Cobb had not given up on bringing the crime home to Thomas Orrock, of whose guilt he had not the slightest doubt. Orrock himself had dropped out of sight and nobody knew where he had gone. One day, the remorseless Sergeant Cobb was talking to some young men who let slip that the previous year they had gone with Orrock to Tottenham Marshes, not far from Hackney, where Orrock had demonstrated his marksmanship with a revolver, which he had brought via *Exchange and Mart* magazine for 10 shillings and sixpence. Cobb got the men to describe in detail where this display of shooting had taken place and then he went to the marshes on his day off, to search the tree that young Orrock had used as a target. He managed to dig out several bullets from the trunk.

The bullet which had killed PC Cole was still being held as evidence and, when compared with the those fired by Orrock, it was apparent that they had all been fired from the same weapon. Now all that was necessary was to track down the missing man himself. Eventually, he was located in Coldbath Fields Prison, which stood where Mount Pleasant Sorting Office in Clerkenwell is now to be found. Orrock was charged with murder, standing trial at the Old Bailey in September 1884; almost two years after the shooting of George Cole. On 6 October, Thomas Henry Orrock was hanged at Newgate Prison.

The murder of PC Cole achieved immortality of a strange kind; one feature of the case that inspired Arthur Conan Doyle to write the very first Sherlock Holmes story, *A Study in Scarlet*, was the chisel found at the scene of the murder, which bore which the cryptic inscription 'rock'. When Holmes visits the house where a murder has taken place, he finds the word 'rache' scrawled on the wall in blood. This mysterious clue is a direct reference to the finding of 'rock' on the chisel, following George Cole's murder.

These two shootings at unarmed police officers were not uncommon during the 1870s and 1880s. The criminal armed with a deadly weapon then, as now, was seen as a dreadful menace. It seemed that the streets were not safe and at any corner one might encounter a dangerous criminal brandishing a pistol. This eventually led to demands for the general arming of the police.

Throughout the nineteenth-century, anybody could walk into a gunsmith's shop and purchase a pistol. Revolvers could be bought by mail order as well, as we saw with the murder of PC Cole in Hackney. There was no system for keeping track of the sale of such weapons and many people kept pistols at home or carried them for protection. Inevitably, with such ready availability, many criminals were also armed. It was not until the *Pistols Act* of 1903 that any attempt was made to regulate or control the possession of firearms in Britain. Even then, it was a slow process. As late as 1968, no firearms certificate was needed for shotguns and any adult could buy a shotgun and ammunition with no formalities at all. There is a powerful and direct correlation between the number of handguns in circulation in a society and the rate of murders by shooting. In the United States, for instance, where firearms are freely available, they feature in over two thirds of homicides. In 2012, 11,000 American homicides were committed with guns; the corresponding figure in the United Kingdom was just thirty five. With pistols freely available in Victorian Britain it should come as little or no surprise that twice as many police officers were shot dead as is the case today.

The wave of shootings carried out against police officers, which became a matter of public concern, began with a murder committed by perhaps the most famous criminal of Victorian Britain; a man who was, in effect, the first celebrity villain. Arthur Conan Doyle, who used the incident from one police murder in his first detective story, mentioned a second police murderer in another Sherlock Holmes story. In *The Adventure of the Illustrious Client*, Holmes tells Watson that, 'My old friend Charlie Peace was a violin virtuoso. Wainwright was no mean artist'. These two are the only real people mentioned in any of the Sherlock Holmes stories. One of them, Henry Wainwright, was a common or garden murderer who killed his mistress, but Charlie Peace was probably the most famous criminal of the era. Including a mention of him in Conan Doyle's story would have given it a pleasing topicality.

In August 1876, a murder took place near Manchester which was, ultimately, to have far-reaching consequences. Three brothers, William, Frank and John Habron, were living and working at a farm on the outskirts of Whalley Range; a small town near Manchester. One of the three brothers, 22-year-old William, was always fighting at the Royal Oak public house and the local constable, Nicholas Cock, frequently ejected him from the pub. As a result of this, there was bad blood between the two men. On more than one occasion, William Habron was heard threatening to murder the officer; once telling him to his face, 'I'll shoot you!' When PC Cock was gunned down in the early hours of 2 August, it surprised nobody that William Habron and his brother, John, were arrested for the murder. Later that year, although the evidence was purely circumstantial, William Habron was sentenced to death for the killing. His brother, John, was acquitted.

Sitting in the public gallery during the trial was a strange looking, middle-aged man. His face was noticeably ugly and he walked with a peculiar spraddle, a consequence of an industrial accident in his youth. Not only that, but one of his arms ended in a false hand; an attempt to disguise the fact that he was missing a finger on that hand.

In the event, despite being sentenced to death, William Habron was reprieved two days before he was due to be hanged and his sentence commuted to life imprisonment. This was fortunate, because he had had nothing whatever to do with the shooting of PC Cock. The man who had gunned down the constable was the peculiar looking character who had, according to his own later statements, enjoyed watching the trial and condemnation of an innocent man. His name was Charles Peace and he was one of a new breed of professional criminals; men who always carried guns and were not afraid to use them if that was the easiest way of evading arrest.

Although the murder of police officers by angry mobs was not an uncommon event in the early years of the Victorian period, by the 1870s, this type of crime was becoming rarer. This did not, however, mean that noticeably fewer policemen were killed. As the death of officers at the hands of crowds diminished, the number of those being shot by ruthless and determined criminals began to rise. Part of this increase was caused by technological advances in the field of firearms. The old, single-shot flintlock or percussion lock pistol had given way to the revolver and this meant that instead of being able to fire one shot and then pausing to reload, it was now possible to fire six shots, one after the other, in quick succession.

The rise of the armed burglar became a matter of great concern to Victorian Britain during the late 1870s and early 1880s. Although the police had many firearms at their disposal, the officer on the beat was still, by and large, armed only with a truncheon. This was clearly not going to be much use when he came up against a vicious man armed with a state of the art, multiple shot pistol.

One of the earliest specimens of this new breed was Charles Peace. A complex man, Peace played the violin well enough to be described in one local newspaper as, 'the latter-day Paganini'; he was also an inventor, designing, among other things, a new type of brush for cleaning railway carriages. His ostensible trade was that of picture framer and dealer in watches and clocks; but really these were little more than sidelines. His real business was burglary.

After serving several prison sentences for burglary and theft, Peace settled in Sheffield in 1872, with his wife and child. From that city, he made forays into Manchester; thinking perhaps that it was safer to carry out his burglaries a long way from where he was living; it was this that led to his shooting PC Cock. While living in Sheffield, he made the acquaintance of an engineer called Dyson. Before long, they became close friends, until Charles Peace began trying to seduce Mrs Dyson. His behaviour became such a nuisance, that the Dysons moved to another area to escape from Peace.

After watching another man condemned to death for a murder which he himself had committed, Peace went straight round to where the Dysons were living in another part of Sheffield and shot Mr Dyson dead. The dead man's wife recognized her husband's killer and before long, Charles Peace was a wanted man. His name and description were circulated across the whole country. This was the beginning of Charles Peace's celebrity status because, despite the large rewards offered for his capture and the fact that every police officer in the country was on the lookout for him, he managed to remain at liberty for the next two years. Not only did he stay free, Peace continued his career as a master burglar; moving back and forth across the length and breadth of England. Hull, Doncaster, Bristol and Bath were all temporary bases for this most resourceful of criminals, before he finally settled in London.

How could the most wanted man in England live openly as a dealer in musical instruments in Lambeth, without anybody recognizing him? After all, his physical appearance could hardly have been more distinctive. The answer is that Peace possessed an uncanny skill at contorting the features of his face. So effective was this, that it was said even his friends and relatives would pass him in the street without recognizing him. Whatever the explanation, for two years Charles Peace set up shop in south London; running his antiques business by day and going out at night in a pony and trap to the prosperous suburbs of Camberwell and Blackheath, where he would loot wealthy homes to his heart's content.

All good things come to an end though and at 2.00 am on the morning of 10 October 1878, PC Robinson, accompanied by two other officers, saw what looked like somebody prowling with a dark lantern on the second floor of a villa in Blackheath. The three officers surrounded the house and in the ensuing struggle to capture the burglar, Robinson was shot. They did not know it, but the man that they had detained was none other than Charles Peace.

Incredibly, even when he was in police custody, not one person identified the murderous burglar correctly and if Charles Peace hadn't made the fatal error of writing to a friend and fellow inventor from prison, they might never have done so. As it was, the man to whom he had written informed the police of his suspicions. Peace was sentenced to life imprisonment for the attempted murder of PC Robinson and subsequently taken north to be charged with the murder of Mr Dyson. Never one to give in easily, Peace jumped from the train during the journey, but was quickly recaptured.

At the Leeds Assizes, Charles Peace was convicted of Dyson's murder and sentenced to death. In view of the fact that he was already serving a term of life imprisonment for shooting another man, there was little hope of a reprieve and commutation of his sentence. That being so, and realising that he had nothing to lose, Peace confessed also to the murder of PC Cock. He gave enough details to persuade the authorities that he had actually been present at the crime and, as a result, William Habron was released from gaol and granted £1,000 compensation for the ordeal he had suffered.

Although he met his death bravely, it appeared to the very last that Charles Peace felt hard done by. During the last visit by his wife, he gave her a memorial card, which he had designed himself to commemorate his death. It read;

In Memory of Charles Peace
Who was Executed in Armley prison
Tuesday February 25th 1879
Aged 47
For that I don but Never Intended

He appeared to see himself more as a victim of circumstance than a ruthless and cold-blooded killer. On the morning of his execution, he was far from satisfied about the quality of the breakfast, remarking to a warder, 'That was a bloody rotten bit of bacon.' Even on the scaffold itself, he complained about the meal, telling the chaplain that the bacon had been too salty.

When the hood had been placed over his head and the rope adjusted, Peace claimed to be thirsty and asked to be given a glass of water. Instead, the executioner operated the trap, cutting short a second request for a drink.

The murder of PC Cock by Charles Peace in 1876 was the first in a spate of police murders by the use of firearms. Four months after the death of Nicholas Cock, two more police officers were murdered in the Berkshire town of Hungerford, one of whom was shot. On the night of 11 December 1876, Inspector Joseph Drewett and PC Thomas Shorter were on patrol together, but went missing on a lonely country road a mile outside Hungerford. They were both found later, the constable beaten to death and the inspector had a gunshot wound to his neck. The following year, 34-year-old Police Constable Henry Cook was shot by a man who was resisting arrest. PC Cook later died of his injuries.

By the time that Charles Peace was hanged, it might have looked to some as though there was a positive epidemic of shooting at the police. In addition to those who were actually killed, there were many instances of officers being threatened with guns or fired at when an arrest was being attempted. Three months before Peace was hanged, another policeman had been shot dead.

One morning in November 1878, Sergeant Jonah Sewell was going about his duties in the Lancashire district of St Helens. He happened, quite by chance, to bump into an 18-year-old youth called Hugh Carey, who was wanted by the police for threatening to kill the foreman of the site where he worked as a labourer. A warrant had been issued for the youth's arrest, but Sergeant Sewell did not have it with him. When he accosted Carey and searched his pockets, the young man pulled out a revolver and shot the police officer dead. He then fled to Ireland, from where he was later brought back to stand trial for murder.

It might have been supposed that there could not have been a more clear cut and obvious case of murder. There was no dispute that Hugh Carey had been the one who had whipped out a pistol and shot dead Sergeant Sewell. At Carey's trial though, which took place in the same month that Charles Peace was hanged, the judge ruled that because the police officer did not have the warrant for Hugh Carey with him, he had no right to stop and search him. Consequently, it was ruled that the charge of murder could not be sustained and that Carey should face only the lesser charge of manslaughter.

Some at the trial assumed that this meant the judge was favourably disposed towards the young man and that he would be given only a nominal sentence. This proved to be very far from the case though, as after the jury brought in a verdict of 'Guilty', Hugh Carey was sent to prison for twenty-five years. In those days, before the automatic reduction of sentences, this mean that the 18-year-old might very well be facing the prospect of remaining in prison until he was forty-three. There were horrified gasps from Carey's relatives when the judge announced the length of time that he would serve.

Just five months after Charles Peace was hanged and young Hugh Carey was sent to prison for twenty-five years, another policeman was shot and killed. 26-year-old PC Joseph Moss was booking an arrested prisoner into the cells at the police station in Derby, when the man produced a pistol and shot the constable.

There was no doubt that more and more criminals were carrying guns and were not afraid to use them when cornered. Then, as now, events in the capital seized the attention of the government in a way that those same incidents might not, were they to take place in the provinces. It was the shooting of a number of police officers in London itself which really made people sit up and take notice. It was one thing for a constable to be gunned down in a rural district in the north of England, but when such a thing happened in Kingston upon Thames or Wimbledon, then it really was time to act. Many believed the only way to tackle such crime would be the routine and widespread arming of police officers on the beat; a step which was eventually taken in the early 1880s.

On the night of 22 September 1881, 23-year-old PC Frederick Atkins was on night duty in Kingston. Part of his beat was along Kingston Hill and as he went along, he checked that the windows and door of some of the larger villas on that road were fastened securely. Atkins was walking up the drive of one house, when he almost bumped into a figure in the darkness. Before the young constable was able to say a word, the man in front of him drew a revolver and fired three times, hitting Frederick Atkins in the stomach, chest and groin. Then his assailant ran off into the night. He was never caught.

The murder of PC Atkins was the catalyst for a public debate about the desirability of routinely issuing guns to policemen on the beat. Letters appeared in the newspapers, questioning the wisdom of allowing men armed only with truncheons to go up against criminals with revolvers, which they were prepared to use at the slightest provocation. *Punch* magazine carried a full-page cartoon, showing a villainous looking burglar pointing a pistol at a policeman who was ineffectually waving a truncheon. The caption to this cartoon was a short poem, supposedly a lament by the police officer:

> *Bar his Colt, there's nought alarming,*
> *To a man, in Burglar Jim,*
> *But if us you can't be arming,*
> *'Ow about dis-arming him?*

Presumably Home Secretary Sir William Vernon Harcourt read *The Times* and the *Daily Telegraph*, in which many of the letters urging the arming of the police force were appearing, because he contacted Commissioner of the Metropolitan Police Sir Edmund Henderson and asked him whether or not the time had come to arm the police.

Henderson consulted with senior officers and came up with two good reasons why this should not be done. In the first instance, he assured the Home Secretary, the men themselves were greatly against the idea. Secondly, it would be a public relations disaster, damaging the image of the police. Sir William was not entirely satisfied with this answer and directed the commissioner to ascertain the wishes of the men themselves. Sir Edmund Henderson went off and in due course produced a memorandum on 'Arming the Police with Revolvers'.

The memorandum submitted to the Home Secretary confirmed what he had already been told by Sir Edmund, who said that his officers had been consulted and were dead against the carrying of revolvers. Not only that, but there were serious legal objections to the proposal. It was thought that there would be a risk of an officer being liable to prosecution, were he to kill a suspect with his gun; a familiar point today, as has been seen in a number of recent cases when the police have opened fire. Instead of issuing pistols, Sir Edmund Henderson thought that it would be better to send the men in lonely districts out in pairs, rather than letting them patrol alone.

The murder of PC George Cole came just a month after the Home Secretary received the memorandum on arming Metropolitan Police officers with revolvers. Police officers were also shot at in Birmingham and pistols were brandished on many other occasions. Then, in the summer of 1883, came two more shootings, which occurred within a few weeks of each other. PC Boanes was on duty in the early hours of an August morning in Wimbledon; a district of south London. He came upon two men, whom he decided were probably up to no good. Boanes arrested one of the men and took his arm to lead him to the police station. At this point, his prisoner pulled out a knife and threatened the officer. The policeman grabbed the man's wrist and almost succeeded in making him drop his knife. So intent was he upon disarming the suspect of the knife, that Boanes didn't notice the man's other hand dive into his coat pocket, from which he drew a revolver and began firing at the policeman. There can be no doubt that he meant to kill PC Boanes, because he fired three shots in quick succession. One bullet hit the officer's hand, another went through his thigh and the third struck his helmet. It was nothing short of a miracle that PC Boanes was not killed. After the two men ran off, Boanes managed to reach a house where first aid was given. A few days after the shooting in Wimbledon, came an even more troubling example of the way in which guns were being used freely on the streets of British cities. The Hamilton House School for Young Ladies was on Anette Road, a quiet street in the North London district of Holloway. On the evening of Saturday, 18 August 1883, the headmaster, Mr Hassell, was sitting quietly in a room on the first floor of the building, when he saw somebody trying to climb through the window. He made a grab at the figure, whereupon the burglar fell into the garden. Mr Hassell shouted for help.

Several people, a number of men and a woman, chased the fleeing man who then turned on them, produced a revolver and opened fire. The woman cried out. She had been shot in the shoulder. The men ran forward and one of them, 39-year-old Harry Hurst, was struck in the knee by another bullet. Then Joseph Kendrick, who lived nearby, was also hit, and the rest of the pursers drew back. The burglar escaped. The fact that a determined and ruthless burglar could open fire in this way without warning, wounding three ordinary people, caused a great deal of alarm, not only in London, but throughout the whole of Britain.

These two new shootings created an air of crisis about gun crime and attacks on the police. The Home Secretary decided it was time to look again at the question of arming officers on the beat and he tried to contact the commissioner. Unfortunately, Sir Edmund Henderson was holidaying off the coast of Scotland in a private yacht and could not be reached. One of the two assistant commissioners had also gone to Scotland on his holidays, leaving the police of London under the control of Assistant Commissioner, Colonel Douglas Labalmondiere. Home Secretary Sir William Harcourt was not at all pleased to find that only one of the most senior offices was to be found in the capital at a time of what he viewed as a grave crisis. Sir William was even less pleased when Colonel Labalmondiere gave his own views on the spate of shootings. His suggestion was that if an officer approached a house where he suspected burglars were at work, he should simply take out his truncheon!

There was, it is clear from the official records, a yawning chasm between the strong views of the Home Office, who favoured the general arming of the police, and the opinions of the senior police officers, who seemed to regard the whole business as a lot of fuss about nothing. By this time, September 1883, the Home Secretary had been trying for two years to do something about what he saw as a serious and indeed scandalous situation; that unarmed police officers were being gunned down regularly across the whole country. Indeed, he appeared to be more concerned about the dangers that the ordinary man on the beat faced than did their own senior officers.

That summer, Sir William Harcourt's patience finally snapped and he managed to get letters to both the commissioner and assistant commissioner, hinting strongly that he wanted them back in London at once. Both men cut short their vacations and returned to the capital. Sir William must have been talking to some ordinary police officers by now, because apparently he knew that the men on the beat were, despite what the commissioner was claiming, very keen to be armed – especially at night, when most of the attacks had taken place. The Home Secretary did not mince his words when writing to the head of the Metropolitan Police. Among other things, according to the permanent under-secretary at the Home Office, Sir William did not believe what he had been told by the commissioner about the rank and file being opposed to carrying revolvers;

In consequence of the recent attack on a Constable by a man armed with a revolver Sir William has called for fuller reports which embrace the opinions of the Inspectors who are more likely to be acquainted with the real sentiments of the men. A summary of their reports has been furnished to the Secretary of State for Home Affairs and has convinced him that the view previously reported to him by the Commissioners was erroneous and that there is a wide spread and general dissatisfaction in the Police with the present means furnished them for self defence.

In plain language, Sir William had caught on to the fact that the commissioners and his two deputies had been leading him up the garden path and misrepresenting the views of the men on the ground! This uncompromising letter went on to say that the Home Secretary regretted that:

With these reports before him disclosing a most serious danger in the Police finds himself unfortunately without the means of personally consulting the Chief Commissioner or Co. Pearson.

The Home Secretary expressed the hope that out of the commissioner and the two assistant commissioners, at least two would always be available to meet with the Secretary of State when an emergency such as this arose.

It is hardly surprising that after such a stinging rebuke, both Sir Edmund and Colonel Pearson thought it wise to cut short their holidays and race back to London. There was another nasty shock waiting for them, because Sir William Harcourt had obviously no intention of trusting their views any longer about the views of the ordinary constable. The main danger to officers were armed burglars operating at night on the outskirts of London, so the Home Secretary wanted the sergeants and constables of the outer London districts to be canvassed for their opinion about the carrying of guns, with a view initially to arming the police after dark.

When the results of the survey of the police officers actually pounding the beat in lonely suburban areas were collated, they must have come as something of a shock to Sir Edmund Henderson. For two years he had been reassuring the Home Office that the average officer wanted nothing to do with firearms, but when they were actually polled, an astonishing 4,430 men out of a total of 6,325 were in favour of being armed at night. In the face of such support from the rank and file, there was little the commissioner could do, other than repeat his fears that an officer who shot a suspect could find himself on trial for murder. On 24 September 1883, Sir William Harcourt gave official backing to the arming of any Metropolitan Police officer on night duty who wished to be issued with a revolver. At first, this was restricted to uniformed officers on patrol in the outer suburbs, but before long the scheme was extended to both the CID and also men in other districts of the Metropolitan area. The era of the armed British police force had arrived.

On 16 October, Sir William Harcourt authorized the Metropolitan Police to purchase 931 Webley revolvers. These were all stamped with the letters MP, for Metropolitan Police and a serial number from one to 931. Sensing a big new market, perhaps correctly anticipating that other police forces would soon follow the Met and begin issuing pistols routinely, the Webley company began producing a line of 0.45 revolvers stamped on the top strap with the words, 'BRITISH CONSTABULARY'.

When the first pistols were issued the following summer, it was to 'men who desire to have them on night duty and who can, in the opinion of the Divisional Officer, be trusted to use them with discretion.' Although it had originally been planned that the issuing of the weapons would be only to those in outer suburbs, the new regulations made it plain that every officer in London could now carry a pistol after dark simply by asking for one.

It was only a matter of time before police officers in more lonely and out of the way spots than the London surburbs of Wimbledon and Muswell Hill should begin asking why they, too, should not be armed. Seven months after the first pistols were issued to men on night duty in London, another police officer was shot dead by a gang of criminals. The murder took place just outside London.

On Tuesday, 20 January 1885, two policemen were travelling in a pony and trap between the Essex towns of Hornchurch and Romford. They were Inspector Thomas Simmons and PC Alfred Marden; both of the Essex County Police. As they neared Rainham railway station, they were hailed by another constable, who said that he had just seen three men getting off the London train, one of whom was a well-known criminal called David Dredge. The inspector went on to Rainham police station to fetch reinforcements, instructing PC Marden to follow the men and see what they were up to. When Inspector Simmons returned with more men, the three were out of sight. Simmons and Marden went one way in search of them, while the other officers went another.

Inspector Simmons and PC Marden found the three men, who ran off when they saw the police. Marden pursued David Dredge, who turned and produced a revolver, threatening to blow his brains out. At that moment Marden heard a shot and realized that Dredge was not the only member of the group who was armed. Another of the men had shot Inspector Simmons and then run off. There was little that PC Marden could do against two gunman and so he comforted Simmons, who told him that he should pursue the men regardless.

All three of the men encountered that day by Inspector Simmons and PC Marden escaped. Simmons lingered on for four days, but the bullet had entered his stomach, torn through his internal organs and come to rest at the base of his spine. There was little that could be done, other than to make him as comfortable as possible while he was dying.

David Dredge was well known to the police in East London as a burglar. He was picked up two weeks after the shooting of Inspector Simmons and charged with his murder. Despite the fact that it had not been he who fired the fatal shot, the police view was that he was guilty of murder under the doctrine of 'Common purpose', sometimes known as 'Joint enterprise', whereby if a number of people are engaged in an unlawful activity and a death results; then all are guilty of murder.

A month after Dredge's arrest, a man walked into a pawnshop in Euston Square and offered for sale a revolver. The owner of the shop was suspicious and sent his assistant to fetch a constable. After a furious struggle, the owner of the pistol, whose name was James Lee, was detained and taken to Platt Street Police Station. He was not searched first, which proved to be a mistake. When they arrived at the police station, Lee took a handful of ammunition from his pocket and threw the cartridges on the open fire. As they exploded, he attempted to use the ensuing chaos to make his escape. He was unsuccessful.

At the trial of James Lee and David Dredge, Lee was convicted and later hanged. Dredge was acquitted of murder, but convicted of threatening to kill PC Marden and sent to prison for a year.

On the day of Inspector Simmon's funeral, the Essex town of Romford was in mourning as the cortege passed through the streets. Almost every shop, as well as many other businesses, closed for the day as a mark of respect for the fallen officer. Hundreds of people lined the streets to pay their respects and show their sympathy for the dead man's family and 2,000 people attended the funeral itself.

After the murder of Inspector Simmons, the Essex Constabulary, took their lead from the Metropolitan Police and approached the Home Secretary to make the case that if officers of the London police were in danger on the edge of the city, then surely the constables of Essex, patrolling lonely lanes in the countryside also needed the reassurance of revolvers at their hips? Sir William Harcourt agreed, and authorized the force to acquire Webley pistols. In June, four months after the death of Inspector Simmons, the police in Essex were also allowed to carry revolvers after dark. The Chief Constable of Essex, Major William Poyntz, ordered that revolvers were to be issued to officers who wished to have them on night duty; provided that the Divisional Officer felt that they could be trusted to use them with discretion.

There was a sequel to the shooting in Essex, one which led to the arming at night of yet another force. Three men were involved in the shooting dead of Inspector Simmons, two of whom were caught and tried. It was widely suspected by the police that the third man had been a career criminal called Jack Martin. It was believed that Martin teamed up with various other men and exploited the railway network to carry out burglaries in different parts of the country. The incident. which led to the murder of Simmonds. began when the three men were seen leaving Rainham railway station.

On 27 October 1885, there was a burglary at Netherby Hall in Cumberland. This was the home of Sir Frederick Graham, a most important man locally, and the police moved very quickly to catch the men responsible. Roadblocks were set up, with the result that the four men who had carried out the burglary were stopped two days later by a sergeant and constable. All else being equal, this would have been the end of the matter, but this was no equal match; the burglars were armed and the police officers were not.

The gang of burglars was led by Jack Martin, the man suspected by Essex police of involvement in the murder of Inspector Simmons earlier that year. The other three men were Anthony Rudge, William Baker and James Baker. As soon as Martin saw that they had walked into a trap, he drew a pistol and fired at Sergeant Roche; hitting him in the arm. Rudge shot PC Johnson in the thigh and then, having broken free of the roadblock, the burglars headed to the nearest railway station.

A little while later, PC Handley stopped the four men and asked where they were going. One of them drew a pistol and threatened Handley, so he allowed them to pass. They walked along the railway track towards Dalston Road Crossing, where they were heard and seen by the man operating the signal box. Soon after this, another police officer came upon the four men and they beat him senseless with their pistol butts. Shortly afterwards, William Baker decided to make off on his own. The other three reached Plumpton Station, where the stationmaster thought that there was something suspicious about the men who appeared at his station, having evidently walked there along the railway tracks. He sent for PC Joseph Byrne, the local constable.

The three suspicious characters had vanished by the time PC Byrne arrived at the station, but he went in search of them nonetheless. A short while later, the stationmaster heard a single shot. PC Byrne had been shot through the head and thrown into a ditch. He was alive when found, but died soon after.

Eventually they were caught, but it was not the police who captured the men responsible for killing PC Byrne and shooting the other officers. There was a hue and cry for the killers and when three men were seen climbing furtively into a goods train at Keswick Junction, a group of railway workers cornered them and relieved them of their guns. All three were charged with murder. William Baker, who had not been with them when Byrne had been killed, was later caught in Manchester and sent to prison for his role in the burglary at Netherby Hall.

At their trial for murder, held at the Carlisle Assizes, Jack Martin, Anthony Rudge and James Baker were all found guilty of murder and sentenced to death. The three of them were hanged simultaneously in Carlisle Prison on 8 February 1886. On the morning of his execution, Jack Martin told Berry, the hangman, 'You hanged Lee at Chelmsford for shooting Inspector Simmons at Romford. He was innocent. That crime was committed by me.'

The murder of police constable Joseph Byrne prompted other police forces to begin arming their men at night. The number of policemen actually being killed by armed criminals might have been low, but there is no doubt that there were quite a few burglars and other criminals who were now ready to open fire if they thought this was the best way to escape arrest. In July 1885, PC Davis was shot and wounded by two burglars whom he tried to arrest near Kensington Gardens, in London's Notting Hill district. That same month, a burglar broke into the home of Israel Rosenblum in Salford, a town on the outskirts of Manchester, and when Rosenblum disturbed the young man, he was shot.

Generally, the process by which various police forces across the country began arming their officers regularly at night was random and haphazard. This was not the case, though, with one section of the Metropolitan Police, who became permanently armed at all times; day and night. These were the Dockyard Divisions, who from 1860 were responsible for guarding the Royal Dockyards, both in London and also at places as far from London as Portsmouth and Chatham.

Even before 1860 – when the passing of the Metropolitan Police Act gave the Commissioner of Police the right to provide constables for the security of all the dockyards in Britain – the Metropolitan Police had already been responsible for guarding the dockyards at Deptford and Woolwich. Very early on, it was thought wise to arm officers undertaking such duties. The Royal Navy was, of course, of enormous importance in nineteenth-century Britain; the 'Senior Service' being the chief means by which the Empire was held together. In June 1854, an order was made for the provision of 113 pistols for police officers on duty at Woolwich. Since there were only 128 officers in total at Deptford and Woolwich, this suggests that most, if not all, would have been armed. This impression is confirmed by photographs taken at dockyards during the second half of the nineteenth-century. Police officers in such photographs, although wearing standard uniforms, almost invariably have military belts around their waists with holsters attached.

The range of locations where the armed officers of the Metropolitan Police Dockyard Divisions were operating, meant that the sight of openly armed policemen was far from uncommon in late Victorian Britain. The majority of police officers carrying guns did so at night, but those guarding dockyards were present during the day as well. At Woolwich and Deptford in London, Chatham in Kent, Portsmouth, Pembroke, Devonport, as well as Purfleet in Essex, armed policemen were to be seen. Their authority extended 15 miles from their bases, so it was not only in the immediate vicinity of the dockyards that one might meet a constable carrying a revolver.

The Dockyard police and ordinary officers on night duty were not the only police to be issued with firearms at this time. In the aftermath of the shooting of Sergeant Brett in Manchester and the explosion in Clerkenwell, many police officers were armed. From 1881 onwards, London became prey to dynamite attacks. It was thought wise to provide armed guards for cabinet ministers and some public buildings; most notably, government offices in Whitehall. This was considered especially urgent after 24 March 1883, when a massive explosion ripped through a street near the Houses of Parliament. As an emergency measure, members of the Royal Irish Constabulary were brought to London to stand guard outside important buildings. These police officers were armed not only with pistols, but rifles too and became a familiar sight in central London. Later on, men from the Metropolitan Police were issued with firearms when they were escorting Fenian prisoners to and from prison. Remembering perhaps the rescue of the Fenians from the prison van in 1867, the officers riding on top of the vans, which transported Irish prisoners from Bow Street Court to Millbank Prison, travelled with their pistols drawn, in their hands and ready at once for action.

There is every reason to suppose that the Victorian public were, towards the end of the nineteenth-century, not at all opposed to the idea of an armed police force. All the reluctance to countenance such an idea apparently came from senior police officers. The wave of attacks in which guns were used against the police or householders was frightening enough for many people to justify such a move.

The use of guns against the police continued, despite some forces being armed at night. On Saturday, 31 July 1886, for instance, PC Alfred Austwick served a summons on a man in the Yorkshire town of Barnsley. James Murphy was a 45-year-old poacher and drunk, who had often clashed with the local constable. After PC Austwick had served him with a summons for riotous and drunken behaviour, Murphy went on a pub crawl around Barnsley. At 3.00 pm that afternoon, he was drinking in the Station Hotel in Barnsley. He told Mr Burgess, the landlord: 'Austwick has served this summons on me. He'll never serve another, because I'll blow a hole in him tonight before I sleep.'

That night, PC Austwick encountered James Murphy, who was very much the worse for wear after a day spent drinking heavily. When he saw the police officer, Murphy darted into his house and emerged carrying a pistol, with which he shot the constable dead on the spot. Following his trial at the York Assizes later that year, James Murphy was convicted of murder and hanged on 29 November 1886.

Gradually, the use of firearms by criminals began to decrease over the next few years. It is customary for sociologists to assert that severe punishments are no deterrent to crime and that it is the likelihood of being caught which influences the decision on the part of a would-be criminal, whether or not to go ahead and take the risk. It is, however, curious to note that just as the garrotters decided to call it a day shortly after they faced the prospect of being flogged as well as imprisoned, so too did the use of guns against the police decline sharply when the police officers on patrol were in a position to shoot back! This may perhaps be coincidental, but that was certainly not the view of the police themselves.

They say that nothing lasts like the temporary and this certainly proved true of the experimental issuing of firearms to officers on the beat. In June 1884, the Home Secretary authorized the carrying of revolvers when on night duty. It was thought that this would be a short-term measure to combat an unprecedented situation. In fact, the regulations remained in force until July 1936. For over half a century, any police officer in London and various other parts of the country could, theoretically at least, draw a gun at any time after dark. In practice, the habit died out long before 1936.

During the 1890s, officers on the beat gradually came to realize that the chances of their encountering a gunman were very slim. Whatever the reason, the spate of shootings by burglars had passed and there was little point in carrying a pistol just for the sake of it. By 1900, hardly any revolvers were issued for night duty in the Metropolitan Police area. Five years later, not a single officer was availing himself of the permission to do so. The British police had flirted with firearms and chosen, in the end, to do without them.

Chapter 7

Black Monday and Bloody Sunday:
Rioting in the West End

T he West End of London is that part of the city extending
roughly from Holborn in the east to Marylebone and Hyde
Park in the west. It includes the main shopping districts of
Oxford Street, Bond Street, Regent Street and Piccadilly, as well as
a number of cinemas, theatres, clubs and art galleries. To the south,
Mayfair and St James are the centre of the West End; with Buckingham
Palace and the Houses of Parliament laying on the edge of the area.

There is something about crime and disorder in London's West End
which seems to grab the attention of the ordinary person far more than
any disturbance on the streets of some provincial town. This is perhaps
because it is the most prosperous part of the capital; world famous for
its commerce and cultural life. For whatever reason, violence in the West
End is always viewed as peculiarly frightening, as a threat to the stability
of the established order. It is almost as though chaos in the West End
is seen as a barometer of the moral state of the nation, indicating when
society is degenerating. In March 1990, for example, rioting began in
Trafalgar Square after a protest meeting about the introduction of a Poll
Tax. Crowds surged across the West End in an orgy of vandalism, arson
and looting. Because of the location of the violence, this event was treated
as being of enormous significance. Perhaps, it has since been suggested,
the Poll Tax Riot was even instrumental in precipitating the resignation
of Prime Minister Margaret Thatcher later that year. It is unlikely that
such a notion would have been floated about rioting in any other part of
the United Kingdom.

Twenty years after the Poll Tax Riot, a series of demonstrations which got out of hand caused similar alarm. Students protesting about the rise in tuition fees rampaged through the West End on several occasions; committing acts of vandalism, starting fires and damaging police vehicles. One group of protestors came, by chance, upon a car in Regent Street, which was carrying the Prince of Wales to an official engagement. The vehicle was surrounded and a group of young men kicked at it, threw paint and cracked one of the windows. This was viewed in the press as a shocking and quite unprecedented thing to happen to such an important person. That this should have occurred in the heart of the West End somehow exacerbated the offence. For many people, the sight of demonstrators, rioters or looters rampaging through London's West End has an almost apocalyptic feel; which would be lacking if the disorder were to be taking place instead in the vicinity of a provincial football ground or around a local public house on a Saturday night. The dismay generated by the Poll Tax riots and more recent student protests, indicate that a lot of people see wholesale vandalism and looting in the thoroughfares surrounding Oxford Street as symptomatic of some modern malaise. It is time now to look at some of the events in the West End during the late Victorian period of the 1880s and examine the circumstances which led to the worst violence seen there for many years.

By the beginning of 1886, Britain had been in the grip of a recession, which had lasted for nearly fifteen years. Unemployment had reached record levels and without a welfare state to cushion the impact of poverty, many families in the poorer parts of the country were, literally, starving. Although well-meaning people launched charitable endeavours to help those worst affected by the economic slowdown, some left wing agitators, the Social Democratic Federation, for example, felt that what was needed was a fundamental reorganization of society on more just and equitable lines. Tariff reform was also demanded; the flow of cheap foreign goods into the British market being blamed by both ordinary workers and some opposition politicians for the rise in unemployment. A rally was arranged in Trafalgar Square by the London United Workmen's Committee, which was intended to draw the attention of the more wealthy to suffering among unemployed and hungry workers. This was scheduled for Monday, 8 February 1886. It had been a particularly bitter winter, the coldest for thirty years. This did not improve the atmosphere among the largely unemployed men attending the rally. Their families had not only been hungry for many months but a lot of them had not been able to afford fuel to heat their homes either.

As is all too often the case today, during the nineteenth-century the police frequently fell between two stools when it came to policing potentially troublesome situations such as the Trafalgar Square demonstration. On the one hand, there were plenty of people ready and willing to accuse them of being heavy handed and brutal in their dealings with a peaceful crowd. Then again, if disorder arose, newspapers were waiting to denounce them for not having made adequate preparations or acted more quickly. In two of the disturbances connected with Trafalgar square in 1886 and 1887, both accusations were made, one after the other.

The meeting in Trafalgar Square on 8 February had been arranged by the London United Workmen's Committee, which was an association of unskilled workers. They were calling, among other things, upon the Lord Mayor to help families in London who were suffering through unemployment. Other concerns were increasing investment, aimed at generating jobs in Britain, as well as stopping the importation of cheaper foreign goods. The police, knowing that this was intended to be a peaceful and law abiding event, sent only a small force to keep an eye on things. Another group, the revolutionary socialist organization called the Social Democratic Federation, arranged to hold a rally at the same time as that of the London United Workmen's Committee. Approximately 20,000 men filled the square and although the mood was serious, it was not aggressive. This changed when socialist speakers began calling for the overthrow of the existing system and denounced not only the government, but all the existing political parties.

Once again, we see an eerie resonance or foreshadowing of more recent events of this sort. When demonstrations descend into violence, it is often because a small band of well-organized militants are thought to have hijacked the original protest and manipulated it for their own ends. These days, it is anarchists or the likes of Class War who are implicated in such activism. In 1886, it was the Social Democrats. Their orators at the meeting in Trafalgar Square that February were not especially interested in tinkering with the capitalist system by means of tariff reform or schemes for alleviating poverty. They believed that the whole edifice of Victorian society was rotten and should be brought tumbling down.

While the speakers on the main platform at the foot of Trafalgar Square were calling for moderate measures, such as the creation of schemes to provide work for unemployed men on public projects, the revolutionaries were making speeches which urged a general workers' uprising. When the question was asked, 'When we give the word for the rising, will you join us?', about a third of the crowd shouted that they would. As the rhetoric grew more inflammatory, some of the listeners began responding in a practical way to the incitement, by seizing well-dressed passers by and robbing them. Then, as the meeting of the London United Workmen's Committee and their supporters broke up, the rioting began.

There are resonances here with several of the ideas which we have already considered. On the one hand is a body of the lowly and dispossessed, those whom Marx described as the *lumpenproletariat*; a German expression for what we call the 'mob'. These were what Marx described as 'the dangerous class'; 'vagabonds, pickpockets, tinkers and beggars'. Such types are all too often to be found on the edge of disorder. Nowhere was this more common than in the disturbances which racked nineteenth-century London. These men have a grievance which does not really relate to either tariff reform or schemes for public works to provide employment. Such things are no more on their mind than Catholic Emancipation was really to the forefront of the thoughts of those taking part in the Gordon Riots a century earlier. These were people at the lowest stratum of the social order, who wished to wreak revenge upon those above them. Whether this was done by mugging passers by, smashing shop windows, attacking the police or looting shops was a matter of indifference to this mob. Their aim was to attack and cause as much harm as possible while they had the opportunity.

The rally in Trafalgar Square had been approved by the police, who maintained a modest presence there. The officer in charge of policing the square that day was 74-year-old Superintendent Robert Walker, who was not really up to the job. He attended the rally in plain clothes and looked so old and helpless that he was soon targeted by a gang of pickpockets, who stole his wallet and watch.

Superintendent Walker decided that only a relatively small number of officers were needed in Trafalgar Square itself, although he arranged for another 500 men to be on standby, if they were needed.

At the end of the rally, most of the 20,000-strong crowd left peacefully and headed east down the Strand. They marched in an orderly fashion, carrying banners aloft, heading back towards the East End. There was some rowdy behaviour as the column marched back to their homes in east London; a few windows were broken and a number of people were robbed in the streets as the body of men made their way through the business district of the City of London. By and large though, this part of the departing crowd conducted themselves with quiet dignity. A sizable minority, on the other hand, perhaps as many as 5,000 men, made off in the opposite direction, along Cockspur Street towards St James. The progress of this group was anything but orderly. As soon as they left Trafalgar Square, they began to smash windows and loot shops.

It is useful to compare this event with more recent incidences of rioting and disorder. During the 2011 riots, it was claimed – not least by the rioters themselves when interviewed by researchers from the London School of Economics – that a large number of those taking part were not motivated by political considerations, but were no more than common criminals. The language used by the reporter from *The Times*, when describing those taking part in the 1886 West End Riots, expresses identical sentiments;

> *The vagabondage of London, apparently associated by some mysterious sympathy, marched up Pall Mall. The men, who were not workers at all, but members of the criminal class, shouted and howled ...*

How the writer of the article was able to distinguish between one shabbily dressed man who was a genuinely unemployed labourer and another who was a member of 'the criminal class', he does not say.

Until now, the violence had been fairly low key, limited to a few muggings and a dozen smashed windows. Once the mob was in the streets south of Piccadilly, however, they became more daring. Here, too, there are uncanny similarities to the actions of looters during the 2011 riots which swept across England. It was observed by those watching television reports of the the looters in 2011, that they seemed to restrict their attentions to shops selling expensive goods. The films show many rioters stealing television sets and games consoles, but no looting of food shops. The subsequent court cases appeared to bear this out. These were not hungry people seeking free food, but rather individuals out to help themselves to whatever they might be able to sell on at a profit. The actions of the mob, which surged along Pall Mall and then up St James's Street and into Piccadilly on the evening of 8 February 1886, was apparently of the same mind. In Half Moon Street, a shop dealing in spirits and cigars was stormed and the stock removed. A neighbouring shop, a hosiers, lost all the silk mufflers and other luxury goods from its windows. Next was a jewellers, where clocks, watches and necklaces were all swiftly spirited away.

Some idea of both the nature of those carrying out the looting and also of the extent of their depredations may be gauged from the subsequent court cases. The police were unable to prevent the 5,000-strong mob wreaking havoc, but they did pick up various stragglers who were laden down with their plunder. At Bow Street Magistrates Court the following day, some of these individuals made their appearance. John Whiteman, a 17-year-old unemployed labourer, is a fairly typical example. He had been involved in the ransacking of two shops, which had between them lost six dozen bottles of whisky, thirty bottles of brandy, a couple of dozen of claret, a quantity of champagne, £100 worth of cigarettes and cigars, four dozen handkerchiefs, sixty pairs of gloves and many scarves. Whiteman was caught later that day, when he tried to sell some of his haul in a pub. Others were caught near Oxford Street with silver candlesticks and valuable jewellery.

As they looted, the crowd destroyed what they could not steal. A luggage shop was ransacked and the trunks carried out and smashed to pieces. A bath was taken from the same shop and thrown into Green Park. While all this was happening, there were no police at all to be seen. It looked to the inhabitants of Mayfair as though the revolution had arrived and that they were wholly at the mercy of the marauding bands.

As a matter of fact, there were large reinforcements only a couple of hundred yards away, while the riot was taking place. Due to poor communications, though, they did not attempt to deal with the chaos which was engulfing Mayfair and St James. A garbled message did reach the man in charge of the 500 officers being held in reserve, explaining that they were urgently needed in The Mall. This is a long, wide avenue, which stretches for half a mile, from the Admiralty Arch near Trafalgar Square, all the way to Buckingham Palace. The obvious fear was that the mob might march on the palace itself. All available men were rushed to The Mall and drawn up into cordons to protect the residence of the royal family.

The main body of rioters were actually making their way not along *The* Mall, but were smashing and looting their way through *Pall* Mall; two or three hundred yards to the north. This simple mix-up, Pall Mall being heard as *The* Mall, meant that only the odd constable patrolling the West End on foot was available to deal with 5,000 angry men, bent upon destruction and theft.

In addition to the theft from shops, the wholesale smashing of windows was carried out. So extensive and systematic was the damage caused in this way, that observers concluded that many of those in the crowd had come prepared with stocks of large stones to throw. A lot of the windows were broken with chunks of flint, which is not to be found in central London. The obvious inference was that this riot was not a spontaneous outpouring of anger from the unemployed and hungry, but had been planned well in advance. In St James's Street, the clubs to which many of the wealthy and aristocratic belonged were a particular target for the fury of the rioters. At Brooks' Club, forty windows were shattered and the picture was similar at other establishments. It certainly appeared that the leaders of the revolutionary Social Democrats, who had initiated the disturbances that day, had some idea where they would lead the mob. It was noticed that men with red flags led the way into St James and the suspicion was that these were the ringleaders.

After they had passed along St James's Street and Piccadilly, the vast crowd surged into Hyde Park, where some of the leaders addressed them again about the inequalities of the society in which they lived. On seeing some grand carriages passing down Park Lane, hundreds of men surrounded them and ordered the passengers out. Once out of their coaches, they were robbed. At this point, a few police constable appeared on the scene and attempted to intervene. They were hopelessly outnumbered and forced to retreat before a hail of stones.

The liveried driver of one of the coaches was stripped and reviled as a lacky of the propertied classes. The attacks on these carriages are reminiscent of the damage caused to Prince Charles' car in 2010; the only difference being that the actions of the rioters in 1886 were far more violent and menacing. Once the coaches were empty, the crowd smashed them to pieces.

In previous chapters, we have examined the idea that riots of this sort are not really 'about' this or that grievance. Rather, they represent a chance for the dispossessed of society to get their own back, for a time, by abusing and attacking members of the middle and upper classes. It is hard to believe that the angry crowds swarming through Mayfair on that February evening were really that angry about tariff reform!

After breaking more windows in Park Lane, the thousands of rioters returned to Mayfair, working their way along South Audley Street. The following morning, the street looked, according to contemporary accounts, as though it had been the scene of a siege. Every shop had been looted and all the houses had had their windows broken.

Gradually, the mass of men dispersed into the night. There had still been no action of any sort by the police and this caused great anger among those living and working in the West End. The letters page of *The Times* on 10 February showed plainly that people felt that both the Home Secretary and the Commissioner of Police for the Metropolis were much to be condemned for letting things get out of hand. They did not mince their words:

Such an exhibition of executive incompetency as was seen in the West End yesterday has not been witnessed in London within living memory.

A few strong bodies of constables posted at strategic points would have made the shameful scenes yesterday impossible.

Sir,- I do not think any reasonable man can feel anything but indignation at the total want of appreciation of the duties of his office shown by the Home Secretary in allowing a mob of some 5,000 to terrorise the inhabitants of London without making adequate provision to check them.

Yesterday trade was at a standstill; today it is as bad. The loss to the community is enormous. Are the loyal and order-abiding people to arm themselves for the defence of their property, or are we to unite as one man in turning out of office a Government which has shown itself greedy of office and incapable of performing its duties? We know there are tried men who are ready to step into their places and sacrifice themselves for the public good.

This then was the bind in which the Home Secretary and police found themselves. If they acted too precipitately, then some will accuse the government and police of being heavy handed and illiberal. If, on the other hand, as happened on 8 February 1886, they wait patiently on the sidelines and trust the protest will remain good natured; disaster may strike. It is a dilemma all too familiar to this country's police forces to this very day.

The looting and vandalism which took place in London on 8 February 1886 became known as the West End Riots or Black Monday. For the Home Secretary and the police, the message was that in future a *laissez-faire* approach to demonstrations in central London would lead to trouble on the streets and, perhaps even more importantly, calls for the resignations of the Home Secretary and Commissioner of Police for the Metropolis. Political rallies in Trafalgar Square were now to be regarded as potential causes of rioting and no chances were to be taken of a repeat performance of the events of Black Monday.

Discontent rumbled on among the poor and unemployed of London throughout 1886 and 1887. Trafalgar Square became, like Speakers' Corner in Hyde Park, a spot to which those wishing to make public speeches gravitated.

On 18 October 1887, a meeting of unemployed workers was scheduled to be held in Trafalgar Square. The police got wind of this and decided to prevent it. When the speakers and audience arrived that morning, they found the square in the possession of the police. When one venturesome soul jumped onto the plinth of Nelson's Column and unfurled a red flag, he was hauled down at once by a couple of burly constables. It was decided to hold the rally, instead, at Hyde Park, to which the police had not the least objection. Mindful of the looting and disorder of Black Monday, the police followed the crowds leaving Trafalgar Square, to make sure that they didn't get up to any mischief.

The meeting in Hyde Park went ahead without any interference. The police withdrew and simply formed up in force at Marble Arch and Park Lane. There was a rumour that attempts would be made to attack the shops in Oxford Street and, in effect, stage a repeat of the rioting which had taken place in that area the previous year. That something of this sort was planned was shown by what happened next. After listening to speeches calling for the government to alleviate distress among the unemployed by organizing a programme of public works to stimulate the economy, the crowd which had originally left Trafalgar Square had swollen, being supplemented by unemployed people who virtually lived in the park. At what looked to the police to be a prearranged signal, the entire mass of men and women suddenly bolted in the opposite direction from the police at Marble Arch and ran towards the exit at Bayswater Road.

A crowd of over a thousand unemployed people raced towards the smart shops of Bayswater. If the police had done nothing and looting had begun, they would surely have been criticized in the press. That this was not just a group of people making peacefully for the park's exit at the end of a meeting was clear from the fact that they were trampling across flower beds and damaging trees as they hurried in the opposite direction from the police guarding Oxford Street.

Mounted police were sent galloping across the grass from Park Lane to the exit in Bayswater Road and these lined up to prevent the crowd from rushing from the park. They were met with a hail of sticks, stones, bottles and chairs. There was a brief battle, in which the police on horseback drew their batons and defended themselves, resulting in injuries on both sides, including three police officers who needed hospital treatment. What some newspapers called the 'Hyde Park Riot' was a low-key affair, but it was a warning signal to the authorities. From that day onwards, the rallies of unemployed workers held in Trafalgar Square were seen as a problem which would, sooner or later, need to be tackled.

By the beginning of November 1887, impromptu political meetings in Trafalgar Square had become a regular feature of life in that part of London. They were also starting to affect other parts of the West End. Unemployed men were sleeping rough in nearby parks and in Trafalgar Square itself. Although the National Gallery, on the north side of Trafalgar Square, was technically free for anybody to visit, it had until then been a fairly middle-class entertainment. Now, organized groups of unemployed men began touring the gallery, much to the dismay of the usual patrons. There was unease about this, but little that could be done. The situation in Trafalgar Square itself, though, was another matter, because it was actually, like the parks of central London, Crown property.

On Wednesday, 2 November 1887, a meeting of the unemployed took place in the square, which was addressed by a number of speakers. These meetings, which were apparently quite spontaneous, had become a daily event. Some exceedingly inflammatory speeches were made. A man called Webb, climbing onto the plinth of Nelson's Column, delivered himself of the following sentiments, which were reported in *The Times* on the following day:

Peaceful methods have not answered so far and it's no use continuing talking about being unemployed and starving. We must act (Loud cheers). We must act with some definite purpose in view. If we are united in that purpose, the press will sink into oblivion and the police will follow, like the abject cowards that they are (Cheers). Let us stand firm and strike a blow like Englishmen.

This sounded, both to the police and the 'respectable' people hearing it, like a call for revolution.

Trafalgar Square was becoming a no-go area for ordinary people and more like the scene of some modern, urban occupation, of the kind that was seen a few years ago around St Paul's Cathedral. Not only were political meetings held there on most days, the benches were occupied at night by tramps and rough sleepers. The police decided to act. Letters appeared in *The Times*, drawing attention to the speeches being made in Trafalgar Square, asking why the police were allowing the open incitement of criminal activity. At first, the police hoped to deal with the problem without using force and thought that simply forbidding people to hold meetings in the square might be enough. On Tuesday, 8 November, Sir Charles Warren, Commissioner of Police for the Metropolis, issued the following notice:

In consequence of the disorderly scenes which have recently occurred in Trafalgar Square and of the danger to the peace of the metropolis from meetings held there and with a view to prevent such disorderly proceedings and to preserve the public peace.

I, Charles Warren, Commissioner of Police for the Metropolis, do hereby give notice, with the sanction of the Secretary of State, and the concurrence of the Commissioners of Her Majesty's Works and Public Buildings, that until further intimation no public meetings will be allowed to assemble in Trafalgar Square, nor will speeches be allowed to be delivered therein, and all well-disposed persons are

hereby cautioned and requested to abstain from joining or attending
any such meeting or assemblage; and notice is further given that all
necessary measures will be adopted to prevent and such meeting or
assemblage, or the delivery of any Speech, and effectually to preserve
the public peace and to suppress any attempt at the disturbance thereof.

   This notice is not intended to interfere with the use by the public of
Trafalgar Square for all ordinary purposes or to affect the regulations
issued by me with respect to Lord Mayor's day.

   Charles Warren, Commissioner of Police for the Metropolis
   Metropolitan Police Office
   4, Whitehall Place, S.W.
   Nov. 8

At a distance of over 125 years, this notice does not, perhaps, strike us as being draconian. Today, we readily accept the need to arrange beforehand with the police, the holding of a rally in central London. We know that if somebody climbs up on to the plinth of Nelson's Column and begins preaching revolution, that a police officer will tell him or her to get down and stop making a nuisance of themselves. In 1887, matters were viewed somewhat differently; both by the police and also the working-class militants whom they wished to discourage.

   Many working people saw the streets and open spaces as their lawful environment. They resented the efforts of the new police forces to enforce their own standards on how people should conduct themselves in public. There was a determination on the part of the ordinary working men and women of nineteenth-century Britain to assert their right to congregate in the Royal Parks of central London. When the police tried to forbid entry into Hyde Park in the summer of 1866, it led to the railings which enclosed the park being torn down. There were claims that this was 'The people's park'and much the same sort of thing happened with Trafalgar Square. Sir Charles Warren's order was an attempt to limit the rights of working people to use public spaces for their relaxation; at least that was how the banning of meetings in the square was interpreted in some quarters.

There had been rallies in Trafalgar Square on a daily basis and when, on 8 November 1887, the police banned any further gatherings, about 1,000 people met in the square. Firmly, but with good humour, the police managed to clear this crowd; only finding it necessary to make a handful of arrests. Some of the agitators behind the regular meetings and speeches in Trafalgar Square claimed that this was part of an attempt to prohibit public meetings generally. As *The Times* pointed out, it was nothing of the sort. Meetings could still be held in any other part of London, including Hyde Park. The legal position was plain, this was Crown property and those sleeping there were technically trespassing. To put the matter to the test, a great rally was called for Sunday, 13 November. It was fairly obvious that the object of this was to defy the police and occupy Trafalgar Square by force.

After the events of Sunday, 13 November 1887, a mythology developed over the years that police had launched a furious and unprovoked assault on a peaceful demonstration, beating people to death and then calling the army in to help suppress the legitimate protests of the people. This idea was fostered by those who felt that a few martyrs might be useful politically. Naming the event 'Bloody Sunday' was little short of a stroke of genius and it is not to be wondered at that others seized eagerly upon such phrase, redolent of massacre and wanton bloodletting. More recently, of course, Irish nationalists have commandeered the term for their own ends and, for most people, 'Bloody Sunday' is now associated with the gun battle which took place in Londonderry in 1972. The reality was very different. As the order issued by Sir Charles Warren made clear, Trafalgar Square remained open for anybody wishing to walk about and enjoy it. Rough sleeping would not be tolerated, however, and the police were instructed to move on men and women who tried to settle down for the night on the benches which lined the square. Public meetings were, temporarily, banned there. Meetings could, of course, continue to be held elsewhere; in nearby Hyde Park, for instance.

In retrospect, the police attitude seems eminently fair and reasonable. In fact, it is pretty much the situation which exists today. Those wishing to hold meetings or rallies in Trafalgar Square must apply for permission and give advance notice to the police. There is a suspicion that those who organized the demonstration for Sunday, 13 November, were actually doing so because they craved attention and hoped for a confrontation with the police. If their aim was really nothing more than a peaceful political meeting, then why not hold it instead at Hyde Park?

By first light on 13 November, the police secured Trafalgar Square and were determined that no meeting of any kind would take place there that day. By 10.00 am, over 2,000 officers were in the vicinity, and mounted patrols were circling the surrounding streets, ready and willing to break up any groups of demonstrators. Hyde Park was open and it had been publicly declared that a meeting could be held there. Other preparations had been made a little more discretely. In the nearby St George's Barracks, a battalion of the Grenadier Guards was standing by, while on Horse Guards' Parade, a regiment of mounted Life Guards was waiting, in case they were needed.

The police were vigorous in preventing any crowds from forming near Trafalgar Square. They were keen to prevent a meeting in the square itself, and they did not wish to see large groups rampaging through the West End. Throughout the day, there were scuffles as the police moved people on and discouraged anybody from hanging around in the vicinity of Trafalgar Square. This policy worked well enough until about 4.00 pm. Nothing that looked like a parade or march had so far been seen in the area, but word reached the police that a column of men were approaching the West End from south London, hoping to cross the Thames at Westminster Bridge and then march up Whitehall to Trafalgar Square. By this time, there were thousands of people crammed into the streets around Trafalgar

Square and as fast as the police cleared one area, the crowds reformed again a few yards away. It was plain that the police alone would not be able to disperse the thousands of men who were now milling around Charing Cross, Cockspur Street, and Whitehall. One or two charges were made by the crowd at the police lines, but still it was impossible for them to get into the square itself.

At 4.30 pm, two squadrons of cavalry began riding along Whitehall towards Trafalgar Square. At their head rode a magistrate. It looked as though the Riot Act was about to be read and the military called upon to clear the streets. It has already been remarked that however much the London mob might jeer at and fight with the police; nothing but admiration and respect was shown for the troops. This was the case even when, as now, it was the intention to use soldiers to support the police. The cavalry rode round the square, not once but several times. It was obvious that this was a show of force, reminding the demonstrators that, ultimately, they might face weapons a little more dangerous than wooden truncheons. Nevertheless, everywhere that the mounted troops appeared, the crowds cheered and broke out in spontaneously applause. Incredibly, they were regarded as being friends of the working men and not their oppressors.

At the same time that the Life Guards appeared on the scene, the Grenadier Guards were marched out of their barracks and positioned along the north side of Trafalgar Square by the National Gallery. They fixed bayonets and stood at the ready. The police, who had been on duty for twelve hours or so, now knew that if things got any worse, the army would step in to help them. As it was, the Riot Act was not read and the troops returned to barracks without taking part in the fighting. It was felt that their very presence was enough to remind both sides in the battle how things stood. They acted as an encouraging sign for the police and perhaps a sobering one for the vast crowds who refused to leave the area.

The main disorders that day occurred not in the vicinity of Trafalgar Square, but half a mile to the south, near the Houses of Parliament. Two columns of protestors were heading towards Trafalgar Square from south London. One group, perhaps 5,000 strong, crossed Westminster Bridge and tried to force their way up Whitehall. The other came through Westminster to meet the rest of the protestors in Parliament Square. There is reason to suppose that although those organizing the demonstration might have been genuinely concerned about such things as freedom of speech and the right to hold public meetings, their march attracted a large number of people whose only interest was to fight with the police and engage in a bit of looting in the West End. This certainly was the impression formed by journalists and the police. Perhaps the best way to decide what was going on is to look at one of the court cases which took place a month later.

Many of those who crossed the river from south London were carrying sticks and other weapons. There can be no doubt that at least some of them had come specifically prepared to attack the police. On 12 December 1887, one such man was brought to trial at the Old Bailey. His name was George Harrison and he was charged with 'feloniously wounding William Williamson, with intent to disable'. He also faced a second count of attempting to inflict grievous bodily harm upon Williamson, who was a police officer.

Evidence was given that Williamson, a plainclothes officer, was attending the march to keep an eye out for thieves and pickpockets who might be operating under the cover of the disorder. He saw a uniformed officer bludgeoned to the ground and went to his assistance. At that point, he was struck on the head with a length of iron pipe, which had been cunningly wrapped in paper to make it appear innocuous. Several people who saw the man wielding this weapon assumed that it was only a scroll of parchment; a petition of some sort, perhaps. The blow struck at Williamson was murderously strong; his ear was split in two and a gash laid open the bone of his skull.

Police sergeant Roger Honey saw the attack and went to Williamson's aid. There was so much blood, that he at first thought the wounded man had been stabbed. He chased after the assailant and saw him drop a knife as he ran. The sergeant caught the man and disarmed him, taking away the iron pipe which he was brandishing.

At his trial, George Harrison was found guilty and sent to prison for what could very easily have ended up as murder, rather than a vicious assault.

Harrison was not alone in coming prepared to attack the police. Two constables were stabbed in the brawling, which took place around the Houses of Parliament, and others suffered broken ribs from being kicked after they had been knocked to the ground. A number of weapons were recovered after the riot, including pokers and pieces of metal, which would hardly have been carried for any reason other than to injure somebody.

The casualties were not, of course, all on the police side. Local hospitals reported treating at least 200 civilians for cuts, bruises and other, more serious, injuries. In the following weeks three people died as a result of the fighting that day; although it is impossible to say whether they were victims of police brutality or were simply crushed by the rioting crowds. Another fatality of the riot had not even been present at the event! Thomas Leversha was a 62-year-old tailor who, according to his wife, had a very timid and nervous disposition. Mr Leversha and his wife lived in Ambrose Street in the south London district of Bermondsey. On the Monday after the rioting in London, Mr Leversha was reading a newspaper account of the disturbances and, his wife said at the subsequent inquest, becoming increasingly upset and agitated at what he was reading. He suffered a seizure shortly afterwards and died. Mr Richard Holt Robinson, a surgeon, told the inquest that he had no doubt that Mr Leversha had suffered, 'a syncope or sudden cessation of the heart's activity' as a direct consequence of reading the exciting account of the riot in Trafalgar Square.

A week after the riot, another great rally was arranged, supposedly to assert the right of people to assemble in public. An indication of how times had changed, in particular the way in which the public perception of the police had changed since the establishment of the Metropolitan Police, almost sixty years earlier, was shown by the number of Londoners volunteering to be sworn in as special constables. Most ordinary people did not wish to see the streets descending into chaos and it was not only the middle classes who felt like this. Among those who came forward to offer their services were market porters and labourers. Nobody, it seemed, was keen to see a mob running wild on the streets of the capital. In the event, the rally on 20 November went off peacefully.

The appetite for violence and disorder on the streets appeared to diminish as the century drew on. It may have been the case that originally the police were imposing a middle-class vision of order on the streets of Britain's cities and that this was resented in some quarters. However, after more than half a century, it looked as though most people had grown to accept that public spaces should be peaceful and decent; that drinking, quarrelling, lovemaking, singing, fighting and other activities of these sorts were better kept indoors and private. Perhaps it is this retreat of some of the less attractive aspects of life from public and their containment behind closed doors which cause us to denounce the Victorians as hypocrites.

Before leaving the subject of rioting, it is amusing to note what one commentator said in the aftermath of the 2011 riots and consider his observations in light of the disorders at which we have been looking in this chapter.

It will be recalled that one of the men who ended up in court after the rioting of 'Black Monday' was a 17-year-old youth called John Whiteman, who had been looting luxury goods from shops in the West End. The offence of which Whiteman was convicted was identical to that committed by many young men and women during the 2011 riots and David Lammy, the MP for Tottenham, where the riots began, thought that he knew what had caused the disorder and looting that summer. He attributed it to the fact that parents no longer disciplined their children by hitting them, for fear that social services might become involved. A natural consequence, at least as far as Mr Lammy was concerned, was that young people become uncontrollable and eventually run riot!

Views like those of David Lammy are typical of people who do not appreciate that civil disorder has been a recurring event in the nation's history; however children are brought up. There was, of course, no lack of corporal punishment in Victorian Britain, both in the home and at school, but it didn't seem to prevent people rioting and looting if the opportunity presented itself. It would be a rash person who blamed progressive education and lax parenting for the regular outbreaks of civil disorder which plagued this country during the whole of Victoria's reign.

Chapter 8

The Dynamiters:
Terrorism in Late Victorian Britain

In addition to the supposed 'modern scourges' of gun crime and rioting, the 1880s were also marked by another type of crime, which we often treat as being a relatively new problem: that of terrorist bombings. In fact, the world's first organized terrorist campaign was launched against this country during the 1880s. Attacks were mounted against many targets, which would also be struck again in the twentieth and twenty-first centuries, by the IRA and Al Quada. These included the Tower of London, Scotland Yard, Houses of Parliament and London's tube trains.

After the terrible explosion in Clerkenwell in 1867, there was a lull of almost fifteen years before the Fenians returned to cause problems in mainland Britain. The mastermind for the new campaign of terror was one of those who was involved in the abortive rising in Ireland during the 1860s, Jeremiah O'Donovan Rossa. He was the leader of a small group who broke away from the Irish Republican Brotherhood and decided, just as the Provisional IRA would a century or so later, that one bomb exploding on the mainland was far more effective, from a propaganda point of view, than anything which took place in Ireland itself.

The first bomb of the campaign came completely out of the blue and exploded at the Salford army barracks near Manchester on 14 January 1881. No warning was given before the attack and four people passing the barracks were injured, including a boy of seven who was so badly hurt that he died two days later.

Two months later, a grand party was due to be held at London's Mansion House. It had been cancelled, but perhaps those who set out to plant the huge bomb outside the Lord Mayor's official home on that foggy March night were unaware of this. At any rate, at 11.30 on the night of Wednesday, 16 March 1881, PC Samuel Cowell was walking his beat through the City of London, when he saw what he at first mistook for a lighted firework. When he investigated, the constable found that the sputtering flame was not a squib, but rather a fuse, which protruded from a large, wooden crate. He at once extinguished it, picked up the wooden box, tucked it under his arm and carried it off to the police station in Bow Lane.

When the crate was opened and examined, it contained fifteen pounds of blasting powder; enough to cause a great deal of damage, had it gone off. It took no great detective work to deduce that Irish Americans were behind the bomb, because in addition to the explosive, the box also held three newspapers; two American and one Irish.

There was a gap of two months before two bombs exploded in Liverpool; one outside the town hall and the other at the city's main police station. The bomb planted at the town hall was prevented from causing much damage, because three policemen actually saw it being planted. This meant that they were able both to catch the men who had lit the fuse and also, displaying enormous bravery, drag the thing away from the town hall and into the middle of the street. Having done this, they ran for their lives and the bomb exploded with tremendous force. Neither this bomb, nor the one which went off at the police station caused much damage and neither was anybody seriously hurt.

The next explosion was at a police station outside Edinburgh. On the night of Saturday, 12 June 1881, an iron pipe filled with explosives was detonated outside Loanhead police station. Loanhead, a small village about 6 miles south of Edinburgh, was a strange target for such an attack and although it was later established that those carrying out the attack were members of Jeremiah Rossa's group, it was never discovered why they chose such a remote and insignificant target. Then the bombings halted for a year and it was hoped that the terrorists had given up. In May 1882, there was another attempt to blow up the Mansion House in London, but not all of the explosives in the bomb detonated and little harm was caused to the building. In June, a Fenian arms dump was discovered in Clerkenwell; not far from the site of the 1867 Clerkenwell Outrage. This contained a huge quantity of armament; 400 rifles, sixty pistols and around 80,000 bullets. Then, nothing more for another nine months.

This must, initially at least, rank as one of the slowest moving terrorist campaigns in history. Over the two years from March 1881 to March 1883, there were only six bombs; two of which failed to explode. Then, at nine in the evening of Thursday, 15 March 1883, an enormous explosion rocked central London. A charge of dynamite had been detonated in Parliament Street, which links Whitehall with the Houses of Parliament. The bomb had been planted outside a new block of government offices, which housed the Home Office, Foreign Office and the Local Government Board. The destruction was widespread, but could have been far worse. Because the explosion took place opposite an empty building site, the force of the blast was largely dissipated. Even so, every window in Parliament Street and far up Whitehall was shattered. Reports suggested that broken glass littered the streets for over a quarter of a mile from the seat of the blast.

Some indication of how powerful this bomb had been could be gauged by the distance at which it had been heard. There was correspondence on this subject over the next few days in *The Times*. Mr W. Leake, sitting at home in Norwood Road in South-East London, wrote to say that he heard the bomb and his house was 5 miles from Whitehall. This was nothing, according to Mr C.H. Davey of Wimbledon, who had heard the explosion while in his house with the windows closed. He lived between 7 and 8 miles from the scene of the bombing. The winner of this strange competition was the enigmatically named Mr

H.E., who had been sitting in a North-facing, first-floor room in Croydon; nine and a half miles from central London. He too had heard the bomb go off.

The attack in Parliament Street had clearly involved a substantial amount of dynamite. That same night, another dynamite bomb was left at the offices of *The Times*. It failed to explode, which enabled the police to see how the devices were constructed. They were more sophisticated than earlier bombs. For example, instead of lighting a fuse, these 'infernal devices', as the press called them, were triggered by cheap alarm clocks. They were the first real time bombs to be used anywhere in the world in a terrorist campaign.

This explosion in Parliament Street, which had struck so close to the heart of government, galvanized Scotland Yard into action. Explosions in Salford were one thing; people blowing up Whitehall and trying to close down *The Times* was something else. In a similar way to the mugging of an MP in the 1850s being taken far more seriously than comparable attacks on ordinary citizens, explosions in Scotland or Liverpool had been treated lightly but when the bombers began operating within a few hundred yards of parliament; it was time to take action.

On 17 March 1883, twelve police officers in London were selected by the Assistant Commissioner to form the nucleus of a new branch of the Criminal Investigation Department. This unit was set up to specifically tackle the Fenian bombers and was headed by Adolphus Williamson. At first, it was intended to call this new section of the Metropolitan Police, the Political Branch, but at the last moment it was decided the title might sound a little too sinister. The name finally chosen was the Special Irish Branch. The word 'Irish' was later dropped, to leave us with the Special Branch that we know today.

The newly formed anti-terrorist unit had an early success, which was devastating to the plans of the bombers. A man known variously as Thomas Gallagher, Bernard Gallagher and Fletcher, arrived from

America in the early spring of 1883. He set up a factory in Birmingham for the purpose of making nitro-glycerine. This explosive, which comes in the form of an oily liquid, is very easy, but extremely dangerous, to produce. The raw ingredients are nothing more than sulphuric and nitric acid, together with glycerine. Unless mixed in precisely the right proportions, nitro-glycerine has an unfortunate habit of exploding prematurely. It is, even when manufactured correctly, very sensitive to heat and can be detonated by a sharp knock. Dynamite is nothing more than nitro-glycerine, which has been absorbed by some inert substance like certain types of clay. It is then far safer to handle and much less likely to explode of its own accord.

Gallagher and a number of confederates began ordering huge quantities of nitric acid, sulphuric acid and glycerine, on the fictitious grounds that they were experimenting with a new method of making paints. The amounts involved were very large, running into many hundreds of pounds. Having successfully turned out a hundredweight or so of nitro-glycerine, Gallagher and his comrades transported it to London on an express train. They filled two rubber fisherman's boots with the substance and put them in a suitcase. This was left in the left luggage department at Euston Station, with the instruction to store it in a cool place.

Police detectives followed the terrorists across Britain and when they judged that the time was right, they seized them all in simultaneous raids. Modern readers might find something eerily familiar with this scenario, of fanatical terrorists cooking up homemade explosives in premises rented under a false name. This sort of activity is one of the current nightmares of the security services, as we saw in the aftermath of the 7/7 bombings of 2005.

The raids in early April 1883 netted the entire stock of explosives that the Fenians had at their disposal. Gallagher and his fellow conspirators were subsequently sent to prison for life. It was hoped that this might signal the end of the dynamiters' efforts and that their leaders in America would now see what a pointless enterprise it was to send men across the Atlantic to be consigned almost immediately to spend the rest of their lives in British prisons.

So far, the Irish-Americans who had been coming to Britain to wage war on the public were not doing a very good job of it. Their bombs had, up to now, been sporadic and largely ineffective. All that changed on Tuesday, 30 October 1883. At a few minutes past eight that evening, a Metropolitan Line tube train was travelling between Edgware Road and Paddington stations. There was a roar, compared by some witnesses to the crash of thunder; to others it sounded like the discharge of a cannon. An explosion had taken place on the track as the train passed through a tunnel. Fortunately, the train had already passed the spot where the explosion occurred, which meant that it was not struck by the full force. Nevertheless, the rear coaches were badly damaged and over fifty passengers were injured, some seriously.

In an eerie foreshadowing of the simultaneous bomb attacks on the London Underground, which took place in 2005, a few minutes after the explosion near Paddington, the District Line between Charing Cross and Westminster stations was also hit by a bomb attack. This one was larger than the blast near Paddington, although it caused fewer casualties. So great was the force of the explosion that although it took place in a tunnel some way from Charing Cross station, the blast wave travelled to the station and blew out plate glass windows in the building at ground level. A few passengers waiting on the platform were knocked down, but otherwise there were no injuries.

At first, it was thought that these two incidents were caused by faulty gas pipes, but it didn't take long to find traces of explosives in the tunnels. The Fenians were back. The reaction of the public was pretty much the same as that of travellers in London following the 7/7 attacks. Men carrying suitcases or bulky parcels on the tube were scrutinized, any hold-ups in underground services caused rumours to spread rapidly about fresh attacks and those with unusual accents were looked at askance.

Nothing more happened for four months and then at 1.00 am on 26 February 1884, an explosion ripped through London's Victoria Station. A large amount of dynamite had been deposited in the left luggage office there, and had been detonated by means of an alarm clock. As it was the middle of the night, there were few people about and only half a dozen or so men suffered minor cuts and bruises. The damage caused by the bomb, though, was extensive. The left luggage office itself was destroyed in the blast and a large part of the glass canopy over the station was also wrecked. Even shops in nearby streets had their windows blown in. An expert from the Home Office calculated that the bomb must have contained at least 10lb of dynamite. Over the next few days, similar bombs, which had been left at left luggage departments at Charing Cross, Ludgate Hill and Paddington stations, were recovered. The timing mechanisms on these devices had all failed.

The method of detonating these bombs was extremely primitive. Each bomb consisted of a charge of dynamite with a revolver fixed nearby and aimed at it. An alarm clock was secured near to the pistol, with one end of a piece of string wound around the winding key of the alarm and the other end round the trigger of the revolver. When the alarm went off at the set time, the key revolved, spooling the string until it tightened on the trigger and fired the gun, thus setting off the dynamite. Little wonder that such a Heath Robinsonesque device was prone to failure.

There was another lull of several months. At some point (nobody seemed to have kept an accurate record of the exact date), a letter was received by the police announcing that the Fenians intended to blow up Scotland Yard itself, targeting the Special Irish Branch. Their bomb would, they said, 'blow Superintendent Williamson off his stool'. Incredibly, a date was given for this: 30 May 1884. It was also stated that all public buildings would be at risk on that same date. As the weeks passed and turned into months, this letter was forgotten. Just another crank communication of the type that unbalanced people send to the police from time to time. A uniformed constable patrolled the street in front of the offices of the CID, but other than that, no precautions were taken.

Just before 9.20 pm on 30 May, a bomb exploded in the basement of the Junior Carlton Club in St James' Square. Two minutes later, there was another explosion in St James Square; this time outside the home of Sir Watkin Williams-Wynn. These two attacks were intended as a diversion, because ten minutes later, there was a devastating explosion right outside the offices of the CID at Great Scotland Yard. The headquarters of the Metropolitan Police were, at that time, housed in a modest building, which had previously been a private house. It faced a public house called The Rising Sun and nearby was a cast-iron men's urinal of the sort once common in London.

Following the explosion at Victoria Station earlier that year, various precautions had been adopted by the authorities in London. One of these was the fitting of wire grills and meshes to prevent bombs being hidden or planted in particularly vulnerable places. London Bridge, for instance, had a number of holes and buttresses. An explosion in close proximity to these weak points might have had the effect of fatally damaging the structure. Grills had been fitted to the bridge to deny access to any bombers. Some thought this a ridiculous over-reaction to the Fenian threat, but it turned out to be a sensible and far-sighted move. The urinals in central London, which had previously been left open all night, had now been fitted with metal gates and covered with netting so that nobody could leave a bomb there at night. Obviously, somebody had managed to plant a bomb there before the urinal was locked up for the night, because this was the seat of the explosion.

A large quantity of dynamite must have been used in the Scotland Yard bomb, because it ripped open the side of No 4 Whitehall Place, which was the building housing the office of the CID at that time.

The next day, reporters on the scene could see right into the rooms which had been occupied by the members of the newly formed Special Irish Branch. Embarrassingly for the police, the files on the Fenians, which had been so painstakingly compiled over the last year or so, were destroyed in the blast. Extensive damage was also caused to The Rising Sun and a number of casualties from the pub required hospital treatment; including a barmaid whose throat had been cut by a flying shard of broken glass.

A fourth bomb had also been planted that night, but it failed to go off. A street urchin reported to the police that somebody had left a black portmanteau bag at the foot of Nelson's Column in Trafalgar Square. Inside were eighteen slabs of dynamite, weighing over 8lb in total. Had they gone off, it is possible that one of London's most iconic monuments would have been destroyed.

There was another long pause before the next attack. It was one which proved the wisdom of all those grills which had been fitted around central London in order to make life more difficult for the bombers. Saturday, 13 December 1884 was the seventeenth anniversary of the Clerkenwell Outrage. Whether this was a coincidence or not, a group of Fenians had chosen this day for what we would today describe as a 'spectacular'; a terrorist bombing designed to garner maximum publicity for the cause. In this case, the aim was none other than the destruction of London Bridge.

To demolish the most famous bridge in the entire country, to make the old nursery rhyme about London Bridge falling down come true, it was necessary to plant explosives at the base of the piers which supported the bridge. Access to these could only be obtained from the river itself and so at a little before 6.00 pm on 13 December, William Francis Lomasney, his brother-in-law, Peter Malon, and a third man called John Fleming climbed into a small dinghy and rowed out onto the Thames near Southwark. They had with them a number of cans filled with nitro-glycerine, with which they hoped to destroy several of the piers of London Bridge and bring the structure crashing into the river.

The trio of bombers who set out in the rowing boat on that dark and windy night faced two difficulties; one of which should have been obvious and the other quite unknown to them. In the first place, nitro–glycerine is horribly sensitive to mishandling and can be detonated by something as trivial as a sharp knock. This did not make it the ideal explosive to be used under the less than ideal conditions of the boat bobbing about in the darkness. The second problem was that the cavities at the base of the piers in which the three men had hoped to place the nitro–glycerine were now covered with metal grills; expressly designed to foil any attempts to plant bombs.

We will never know what the men in that dinghy decided when they discovered the security grills. Perhaps they tried to place the cans of explosives on some other point of London Bridge. Perhaps they did not get that far and one of them lost hold of a container full of one of the deadliest and most unstable high explosives known to man. Whatever the explanation, at a few minutes past 6.00 pm, an explosion shook the bridge and nearby districts. The police could not at first work out what had happened and thought that a bomb had exploded on the bridge, rather than beneath it. When signs of damage were found beneath London Bridge, the police offered a reward of £5,000 for information that could lead to the arrest of the culprits. Over the next few weeks, it became apparent that they would not have to pay out this generous offer. Literally, piece by piece, the remains of the three bombers were washed ashore at various places.

During the month following the attempted bombing of London Bridge, the terrorists returned to the underground. On the evening of Friday, 2 January 1885, a bomb exploded in the tunnel between Kings Cross and Gower Street Station; which is now known as Euston Square. It was not particularly large despite exploding near a train, only the glass in the carriages was broken and no injuries were caused, other than a few cuts and scratches. Because the police were on the alert for further tube bombings, they already had officers posted at Gower Street. They closed the station and began to interview every passenger on the train, which pulled into the platform after the bomb had gone off. Superintendent Williamson, head of the Special Irish Branch, soon arrived on the scene.

As the passengers from the tube train were screened, one man in particular stood out. He was a young Irishman, who seemed very nervous. He gave his name as Cunningham and provided what later turned out to be a false address. However, all the lights in the station had been blown out and there was a good deal of hysteria, which allowed this man to slip away. Mr 'Cunningham', whose real name was James George Gilbert, reappeared three weeks later.

The climax of the dynamite attacks that were carried out by the forerunners of the IRA came on Saturday, 24 January 1885. Public entry to the Tower of London was free on Saturdays, so it was usually very crowded. More to the point, nobody had any reason to look closely at anybody walking through the gates of the Royal Palace. At almost precisely 2.00 pm, the armoury in the White Tower was shattered by an explosion. Guessing what had happened, the Beefeaters secured the exits to the whole of the Tower of London at once. It was a fair bet that the bomber was still inside the place. This prompt action allowed the police, who had quickly been summoned, to question every single visitor that day. 22-year-old James George Gilbert had an Irish accent and attracted their attention almost immediately. When questioned, he gave his real name but a false address. By a stroke of ill fortune for him, the police officer who was questioning him knew the part of London where Gilbert claimed to live very well. It only took a few questions to establish that James Gilbert was lying about his address. A quick search of his pockets revealed where he really lived.

At the same time that the bomb exploded at the Tower of London, two bombs went off at the Houses of Parliament. One was a small device, presumably intended to set the crowds of visitors fleeing in panic. The other, planted in the chamber of the Commons, was larger and caused considerable damage. Two police officers were seriously injured by the explosions.

A search of James Gilbert's lodgings brought forth a mass of incriminating evidence, including detonators which could only be used for setting off charges of dynamite. An associate of Gilbert's called Henry Burton was arrested, which led officers of the Special Irish Branch to a house in Harrow Road, West London. There, they found a haul of over 50lb, half a hundredweight, of dynamite.

Even though no-one was killed by their bombs, both Gilbert and Burton very nearly faced the death penalty. When the police formulated the charges against the two men, a law officer for the Crown informed them that the Tower of London was officially a royal palace and that an attack upon it could be construed as high treason. It was decided not to pursue the charge; principally because it was in nobody's interest to create martyrs for the Fenian cause. A compromise was reached and the charge against Gilbert and Burton was one of Treason Felony, which was not a capital crime. The indictment charged that the two men had been:

Feloniously conspiring with other persons whose names are unknown to depose the Queen from her Royal name and style of Queen of Great Britain and Ireland. Also for conspiring to levy war against the Queen with intent by force and constraint to compel her to change her measures and to intimidate and overawe the House of Parliament.

The advantages of such a charge, rather than the specific offence of planting bombs in one particular place, enabled the Crown to produce evidence of the campaign generally, rather than limiting themselves to the specific bombings for which the two men had been arrested. When Gilbert and Burton stood trial at the Old Bailey on 20 April 1885, various other explosions were mentioned, such as the one at Victoria Station. Both men were convicted and sent to prison for life.

The Irish were not the only ones detonating bombs in this country during the closing years of Queen Victoria's reign. There was another group of people who were viewed with even greater fear. This was an international terrorist group whose aim was the destruction of the entire way of life enjoyed by the citizens of the liberal democracies of Western Europe and the United States. These were people who despised the very idea of democracy and were quite prepared to sacrifice their own lives in order to attack a system, which they thought of as decadent and corrupt. They set up their bomb factories in the communities of foreigners who had taken root in Britain's larger cities and were responsible for the first fatal bomb attack on the London Underground. They were the anarchists who sought asylum in this country from the 1880s onwards.

By 1894, there was widespread unease about the unrestricted immigration to Britain of people from Eastern Europe. Many of these immigrants could not speak English, or so it was said, nor could they understand the 'British' way of life or hold the same values as those who had been born in Britain. The government was urged to tighten up porous borders and reduce the supposed flood of foreigners entering the country. Europe was shaken at this time by bombs thrown by anarchists. It was feared that if Britain was not careful, that sort of activity might spread to the United Kingdom. On 7 November 1893, two bombs were detonated at the Liceo Opera House in Barcelona, killing twenty-nine people and injuring many more. Three weeks later, Auguste Vaillent, a French anarchist, threw a nail bomb into the Chamber of Deputies in Paris; the French equivalent of the House of Commons. On 3 February 1894, Vaillent went to the guillotine for his act of terrorism and nine days later a revenge attack was carried out at the Gare St Lazare railway station in Paris. One woman was killed and twenty injured in the bombing. The British were determined to avoid any attacks of this kind in their own country.

At about 4.45 pm on 15 February 1894, two workers at the Royal Observatory at Greenwich were finishing some rather complex calculations before going home. Mr Thackeray and Mr Hollis had almost completed their work, when they heard an explosion, which sounded very close. They ran out of the observatory to investigate and saw a park keeper and several schoolboys pointing at the path leading up the hill to the observatory. A column of smoke drifted up from a point roughly midway along the path. A man lay there, dreadfully injured, with his legs shattered and one arm and much of his torso missing. More than fifty pieces of flesh and bone were later recovered from the surrounding park, including a 2 inch-long piece of bone, which had been blown 60 yards.

The injured man was taken to hospital, where he died almost immediately. He was a Frenchman named Martial Bourdin, and was well known in the anarchist circles of London. For reasons that can only be guessed, he had been carrying a can full of nitro-glycerine up the hill towards the observatory. Most probably, he stumbled or dropped the can, whereupon the notoriously sensitive explosive had gone off.

When they searched the dead man's lodgings, police found a bomb factory, with bottles of sulphuric acid, various chemicals and detailed instructions in French for manufacturing time bombs. Their discoveries were leaked to the press, along with the information that the Special Branch had at times had him under observation. Questions were asked as to why more attention had not been paid to a man who was clearly a dangerous terrorist, but the whole incident gradually faded into memory. It was immortalized only in the plot of Joseph Conrad's novel, *The Secret Agent*; which centres around an attempt to blow up Greenwich Observatory.

A month after the explosion at Greenwich, there began a series of bomb attacks on post offices in South London. The first of these was on the night of 14 March 1894, when a bomb exploded at the post office in New Cross Road. There were other, similar attacks in the summer of that year but, as suddenly as they had begun, the bombings of post offices ended. Nobody was hurt by any of these devices.

Nobody was arrested for the post office bombings until February 1897. On 24 January, a plainclothes officer attended an anarchist meeting in Deptford and had been struck by the suspicious knowledge of explosives by Rollo Richards. Richards was 36-years-old and, unlike most of the anarchists at the meeting, he had been born in Britain. As is often the case with converts to a cause, he showed himself to be a little more extreme than most. When the police raided his house on 6 February, they found evidence that he had been making bombs there.

On 5 April 1897, Rollo Richards appeared at the Central Criminal Court charged with, 'Feloniously causing an explosion by gunpowder, likely to endanger life.' The evidence was clear and overwhelming. Richards had apparently spent some time in a lunatic asylum and it was hinted that some of his comrades had encouraged him to manufacture and plant his bombs. He was sent to prison for seven years.

Three weeks after Rollo Richards was sent to prison for his bombs, a Metropolitan Line train pulled into Aldersgate (now Barbican) tube station. As the carriage doors opened, there was a loud bang and one of the first-class carriages was blown to pieces. Fortunately, there had been nobody in that particular carriage, but so powerful was the blast that a dozen passengers in an adjoining carriage were seriously enough injured to require hospital treatment. Not only was that train damaged, but the windows were broken in another one which was standing on the opposite platform. The glass canopy above the platforms was also shattered, raining pieces of broken glass down on those standing below.

Most of those injured by the explosion at Aldersgate Station suffered only superficial cuts. One man was less fortunate. Harry Pitts, a 36-year-old manual worker from Tottenham, died that night in St Bartholomews Hospital; the first fatal casualty to result from a tube bombing in London. Investigations revealed that a bomb using dynamite had caused the explosion at Aldersgate Station on Monday, 26 April 1897. The motive for the attack was unknown, although it was hypothesized that the bomb had been planted in retaliation for the jailing of Rollo Richards at the Old Bailey a few weeks earlier. It proved to be the last terrorist attack in this country to take place during the nineteenth-century.

During the final years of the Victorian era, the streets of Britain were certainly more peaceful than they had been at the beginning, but that did not mean that the police were completely in control of public spaces; nor that the army was no longer called in to help restore order. Discontent at the social system still simmered away beneath the surface, ready to erupt if the circumstances were right. This could happen at sporting events, celebrations or even something as innocuous as a parade by a Salvation Army band.

Chapter 9

The End of an Unruly Era: Disorder and Violence as Victoria's Reign Drew to a Close

The Dickensian image of the nineteenth-century cherished by so many people today, should by now have been comprehensively dispelled. Indeed, the mugging, rioting, gun crime and terrorism of Victorian Britain seems largely indistinguishable from our own age; except that it was, in many cases, a good deal worse than that which we see today. The violence which erupted on the streets of Victorian Britain often had its causes in the most trifling of incidents. A man might be arrested for drunkenness, his friends and neighbours object and in next to no time a 'Freedom riot' could erupt, in which police officers could be assaulted or even, in extreme cases, killed. These sudden outbreaks of ferocious violence were something of a *leit motif* of the Victorian period. The supposed motives for violent disorder might be a strike, a meeting to demand relief for unemployed workers; even something as insignificant as an over-zealous policeman arresting somebody for horseplay in the street.

By 1880, modern police forces existed across the whole country. The streets were beginning to accord with the middle-class vision of clean, safe and orderly urban environments. Nevertheless, trouble was still bubbling below the surface of Victorian society and it needed very little to bring it forth. Some of these disturbances were triggered by events that were, on the face of it, joyful celebrations; times when, theoretically at least, everybody should have been filled with cheerfulness and good will. A couple of truly extraordinary outbreaks of rioting, give some indication of the underlying mood of resentment and incipient rebellion, which was never far away in Britain at this time.

The seaside resort of Worthing, on England's south coast, has for many years been a byword for quiet gentility. It is thought to be less vulgar and brash than the neighbouring town of Brighton. In 1884, Worthing was becoming a popular location both to spend seaside holidays and also to visit for a daytrip. It had all the amenities a city clerk spending a week on the coast could hope for: a pier, ornamental gardens and, of course, any number of hotels and public houses. In the early spring, a branch of the Salvation Army was established in Worthing. These days, it is hard to imagine anything less threatening and provocative than a Salvation Army parade, but things were a little different in the early years of their existence.

The prosperity of Worthing was founded upon the tourist trade. Day trippers and holiday makers spent freely in the town, especially in the pubs. The Salvation Army was, of course, opposed to the sale and drinking of intoxicating liquor and this brought them into conflict with the licensing trade. They were not hugely popular with most of those living in Worthing either. Their parades appeared to be noisy and vulgar and it would be ruinous if passers by listened to their message and signed the pledge to refrain from intoxicating liquor. As in other towns, a group of men, financed by local publicans, formed to break up Salvation Army meetings and marches. These rowdy elements were known in southern England as the Skeleton Army. At first, attacks were limited to throwing paint and rubbish at the smartly uniformed Salvationists. When this didn't discourage the evangelical Christians, tougher tactics were employed.

By July, skirmishes between the Salvation Army and the Skeleton Army were regular events on the streets of Worthing. Most people blamed the Salvation Army for making a nuisance of themselves in the first place. People coming to the town for the day wanted to relax on the promenade on Sunday afternoons; not listen to a lot of noisy hymns! Popular opinion was definitely on the side of those opposed to the Salvation Army. Even the local magistrates were making scathing remarks about the, 'desecration of the Sabbath', which the Salvationists were causing.

On 19 August 1884, there was a near riot, with the Skeleton Army threatening to smash up the shops and homes of supporters of the Salvation Army. A crowd surrounded the shop belonging to George Head, a prominent local man who had rented premises to the Salvation Army. At first, all the windows were smashed by stones, then the door was kicked in, a group of men entered the shop and began trying to burn it down. Since George Head and his family lived over the shop, he tried to prevent this by warning the men that he was armed. When they refused to leave, he opened fire with a revolver, wounding two of the attackers. The police, meanwhile, were quite unable to deal with the situation. Over 1,000 people were milling about in the street outside George Head's shop, but there were only eight officers to man the local police station. They made some arrests but could not restore order. As it was, the shooting at the crowd made the others nervous of continuing to attack Head's shop and so they gradually dispersed.

Things were bad enough that day, but they were to deteriorate sharply the next. Some of the men arrested appeared in court, charged with assaulting the police. The magistrates, having tolerated, and even encouraged, strong opposition to the Salvation Army only a few months earlier, now decided to take a tough line with the Skeleton Army. They sent six men to prison for fighting with the police. By this time, thousands of men were surrounding the court and police station, demanding that the prisoners be freed. When this was not done, stones were thrown, smashing all the windows in the police station, as order descended into chaos. That classic Victorian phenomenon, the freedom riot, once more made its appearance.

By the evening, it was obvious that law and order were breaking down entirely in Worthing, and the chair of the magistrates, Lieutenant-

Colonel Wisden, sent a message to the barracks at Brighton, asking for urgent military assistance. Three hours later, a column of cavalry entered Worthing; forty troopers of the Royal Irish Dragoons, accompanied by three officers. Lieutenant-Colonel Wisden read the Riot Act and the troops, backed by police officers and special constables who had been sworn in that day, eventually managed to clear the streets.

It seems incredible today that Salvation Army meetings in a nice seaside town like Worthing could have ended with the reading of the Riot Act and use of cavalry to restore order, but such was the wafer-thin veneer which separated good order from anarchy at this time. The slightest thing could tip the balance and signal a descent into chaos.

Three years after the extraordinary events at Worthing, a riot took place in London over an even more insignificant occurrence than the Salvation Army singing a few hymns on a Sunday afternoon. Not far from Stamford Bridge, the home ground of Chelsea Football Club, used to be the Lillie Bridge Grounds; a popular Victorian sports ground. The first ever amateur boxing matches were held at Lillie Bridge in 1867, with the trophies supplied by the Marquess of Queensberry. The Middlesex Cricket Club (MCC), was based at Lillie Bridge for a time and it was also the home of the Amateur Athletics Association. The FA Cup final was held there in 1873. All in all, Lillie Bridge Grounds was an exceedingly important sporting venue.

On the evening of Monday, 19 September 1887, a race between the champion short distance runner of the day, a man called Hutchens, and a challenger from the north of England was due to take place. The crowd numbered over 10,000 and betting was lively. The runners appeared and then vanished again. For reasons unknown, the two men chose not to run that day and simply left the ground with no announcement being made. The bookies also melted quietly away. All those present had paid to attend the race and when it gradually dawned upon them that there would be no race, the mood turned ugly. In the words of *The Times*, when reporting on what happened next;

A riot of formidable dimensions which broke out yesterday at the well-known Lillie Bridge grounds proves with what facility the underlying forces of disorder can upon occasion burst through the crust of social conventions that looks so comfortably solid.

Whoever wrote the account in *The Times* was well aware of how easily violence could break in the outwardly safe and well-ordered society that was late Victorian Britain.

Once the men who had come to watch and bet on the race realized that it would not be taking place, they became angry and demanded their money back. When this was not forthcoming and it became apparent that the bookies had also decamped with their stakes, the crowd went berserk and systematically destroyed the sports ground. They began by pulling up the fences and burning them. The four police officers on duty tried to intervene and were badly beaten. One, Sergeant Edwards, had his front teeth knocked out. The stand was smashed up and the seats added to the bonfires, before the mob turned its attentions to the changing rooms and refreshment pavilion. After looting the pavilion, that too was torched. The fire brigade arrived, but when they attempted to put out the fires, they had to retreat under a hail of bricks, bottles and pieces of wood. It was only when police reinforcements arrived that baton charges managed to clear the ground of the rioters.

Lillie Bridge, one of the most popular sporting venues in London, never recovered from the damage caused during the 1887 riot. It closed for good a year later. This riot, following the cancellation of a race, illustrates perfectly the precarious nature of society at this time. It took very little indeed to tip the balance and turn civilization into barbarism. The attitude of *The Times* is worth noting here. Although condemning the disgraceful violence, the report tacitly assumed that rioting would flare up as a matter of course, given the right circumstances. After relating the non-appearance of the runners and the disappearance of the bookmakers, the journalist observed that, 'When a crowd is treated in this fashion, a riot is inevitable ...'

In the two incidents above, which both took place less than twenty years before the death of Queen Victoria, the angry mobs did at least have some cause for complaint. The reactions of the crowds in Worthing and at Lillie Bridge might have been grossly disproportionate, at least by modern standards, but it is indisputable that they felt aggrieved or wronged in some way. During an occasion of national rejoicing when the entire country was celebrating and one would have supposed that the mood of all those people taking part in the festivities was uniformly cheerful and good natured. Even under such circumstances, the danger of violence and disorder was lurking just below the surface.

The Second Boer War, which took place in South Africa between 1899 and 1902, was something of a shock to the British. The discovery that the British Army was not invincible on the battlefield was a sobering one and when, after seven months of war, victories were finally reported, the excitement in this country was unbounded. There was singing, dancing and street parties when the relief of the beleaguered city of Mafeking was announced in the newspapers. Indeed, a new word was coined to describe the exhilaration exhibited by crowds upon hearing the breaking of the siege of Mafeking. 'Mafficking' is defined as the boisterous and uncontrollable rejoicing of people when receiving long-awaited good news. Similar enthusiasm greeted the relief of Ladysmith and the capture of the city of Pretoria.

Celebrations of these military successes developed unexpectedly in some of the quieter and more staid corners of the country, such as the London suburb of Ilford.

Ilford was a fairly well-to-do district to the east of the capital; there were no slums or discontented peasantry to be found there. The houses were modern, there was full employment, and, when news came on the evening of 18 May 1900 of the relief of Mafeking, there was a spontaneous outpouring of joy. The siren of the local paper mill, which provided much of the local employment, sounded for ten minutes and people gathered at Ilford Broadway, the centre of the area, to celebrate by singing patriotic songs. Fireworks were set off and the streets were thronged with happy groups of men, women and children until 3.00 am.

The following month, the Boer capital of Pretoria fell to the British forces. This signalled an outbreak of even more merrymaking on the streets of Ilford; bonfires were lit in the middle of the road in various side streets. The police moved in to put a stop to this, whereupon the crowds outside the railway station at Ilford Broadway went one step further. They began to tear down the wooden shutters from closed shops and light an enormous bonfire in the middle of the main road passing through the broadway, bringing traffic to a halt. The crowds were so great, that the police could not get to this new fire, whose flames were now leaping above the rooftops. A builder's merchant was looted and a cartload of timber added to the fire, which was now threatening to get out of hand.

When the fire brigade arrived at Ilford Broadway, they were jeered and the vehicle rocked to and fro and almost overturned. The hoses were slashed and the equipment badly damaged. While all this was going on, the police were utterly helpless; there was simply too many people for them to be able to tackle the disorder. The crowds did not disperse until 2.00 am.

The next evening, people began to gather once again at Ilford Broadway as it grew dark. A new bonfire was lit in the ashes of the old, but this time the police were ready. Some venturous souls gathered at Clements Road, one of the side streets leading off the High Road, and tried to loot floorboards and scaffolding from a building site. A mounted police officer was waiting for them. As the people trying to get the blaze going became increasingly bold, the police struck. They had drafted in reinforcements; mounted police who charged any groups that looked as though they were up to mischief. It was later alleged that the police lashed out at anybody in reach of their batons. Whatever the truth, the police managed to maintain order that night.

The pretty Warwickshire market town of Stratford-upon-Avon was another unlikely venue for the eruption of street violence. Events spiralled out of control there too after the news of the relief of Ladysmith, which took place on 27 February 1900.

News of the breaking of the Boer seige of Ladysmith reached England on 1 March. In Stratford-upon-Avon, the trouble began when a few young men left the Conservative Club in high spirits and began singing patriotic songs in the street. Passers by joined in and a crowd slowly formed in the high street. The mood was cheerful and triumphant, but as the evening drew on thoughts turned to local tradesmen who had not been supporters of the war; including Henry Bullard, who had allegedly displayed a Boer flag in his shop window. The plate glass window of his shop was smashed and his door kicked in as some men pushed into his premises; a brief fight ensued before they were ejected. The mob became increasingly disorderly as it moved on to Arden Street, where another shop window was kicked in and the windows of a supposedly Boer sympathizer were also broken.

The following night, Friday, 2 March, the mob assembled again and roamed across the town, breaking windows and vandalizing the property of those accused of not having supported the war wholeheartedly. The rioting lasted for about three hours on the Friday evening and began again the next day. The Chief Constable of Warwickshire, Captain Brinkley, came to Stratford-upon-Avon for himself to see how serious the disturbances were. By now, thousands of people were gathering in the streets as darkness fell and the sound of breaking glass was heard all over the town. Captain Brinkley called in reinforcements from other parts of the county and the trouble died down as swiftly as it had started.

The crowds in both Ilford and Stratford-upon-Avon were supposedly celebrating a joyful event; a victory of the British Army. Nevertheless, with feelings running high, the desire to cause damage and start fires was always there, simmering just below the surface.

The disorder in East London and Warwickshire had not been so extensive or violent that the police alone were unable to handle it. There is, however, another example of rioting provoked by victory celebrations where the police found themselves out of their depth. Jersey is the largest, and most populous, of the Channel Islands. Although it is part of the British Isles, it has always had a slightly Gallic flavour, due to its close proximity to France. When news of the relief of Mafeking reached St Helier, the chief town of Jersey, the citizens went as mad with excitement as elsewhere in the kingdom. An impromptu parade was organized, which wended its way through the streets of St Helier with much singing and cheering. Apparently a French woman, called Cousinard, tipped some dirty water from her window onto the crowd; whether by accident or design, it is impossible to say. This was the only spark needed to provoke a peaceful and law-abiding group of men and women into a riotous crowd.

At first the police did not know how to respond to the sudden and dramatic change of mood. One moment, everybody was singing music hall songs and the next, windows were smashed and bricks hurled at the police. They drew their truncheons, but found that there were too few of them to be able to disperse what was now an angry and threatening mob. The next day, the Mayor of Jersey issued an order forbidding gatherings of any description. This did no good, because that evening, crowds began to form again and the windows of those thought to have been opposed to the Boer War were smashed. The victims of these attacks were mainly French inhabitants of the island.

For some reason, the groups of angry men and women congregated outside the home of the mayor and the few police present found that there was little they could do to move the people on. It was at this point that military assistance was called for. Units of the Devonshire Regiment stationed on Jersey arrived and, incredible to relate, fixed bayonets and charged the rioters. There were no injuries, but the crowd fled at once and that was the end of the rioting in Jersey.

Rioting and disorder in Britain was not limited to the early years of Victoria's reign and neither was it a phenomenon of the slums. Disorder was just as likely to occur in respectable London suburbs or pretty country towns as it was in the rookeries of the larger cities. Throughout the whole of the Victorian era, violence was always simmering below the surface and even a supposedly joyful occasion such as the celebration of a British military victory could be enough to trigger rioting.

Epilogue

The Victorian era is a period of British history lasting a little over sixty years and one we think we know well; at least we all have strong mental images of how we imagine Victorian society to have been. It is surprising to discover that the Victorians were facing much the same problems then that we are experiencing today. It's difficult to believe that there was an epidemic of gun crime that led to the widespread arming of the police and a campaign of terrorism that included a series of bombings on the London Underground. When the British media report incidents of violent crime and disorder in modern society, these are often seen as unprecedented, prompting cries of: it certainly wasn't like this when we were children! Any riot is an alarming indication that the fabric of our society is cracking; armed police are a sign of the times; the threat from terrorism is a constant worry, as is the fact that anybody walking about in the larger cities later at night is liable to be assaulted or robbed.

As far as violent crime is concerned, this tendency to hark back to a mythical, virtually crime-free, Golden Age can result in something quite invidious. Persuading ourselves that street robberies, shootings and terrorism are all recent innovations in British life, there are those who may, subconsciously, lay the blame upon those whose parents were not born in this country. In short, they fall into the trap of believing that there is something not quite 'British' about gun crime, gangs, terrorism and looting.

London districts such as Dalston and Clapton in Hackney, which are today associated with black, gang related gun crime, are also mentioned in Victorian newspapers for much the same type of offence; almost a century before large scale immigration to Britain began. Similarly, urban rioting did not begin a few decades ago in predominantly black areas, such as Brixton and Tottenham, but has been an enduring feature of British life for centuries. Events like the murder of PC Keith Blakelock in Tottenham in 1985, far from being some alarming new phenomenon in this country, were actually fairly common in the early years of Queen Victoria's reign. So too with the planting of bombs on the London Underground. This is not a frightening new crime perpetrated by disaffected Muslim youths; it has been around for many years. 1883, 1897, 1913, 1939, 1973, 2005; whether committed by Fenians, anarchists, suffragettes, IRA or Islamists, this too is another feature of life in Britain which has been with us for the last 150 years or so.

Civil disorder, terrorism and violent crime have always been with us; despite our best efforts to create for ourselves an imaginary world in which our country was never plagued by such undesirable things. Over 2,000 years ago, the prophet Ecclesiastes said, 'Do not ask why things were so much better in the past, it is not an intelligent question.' This is still sound advice.

Bibliography

Bloom, Clive. *Restless Revolutionaries, A History of Britain's Fight for a Republic,* Stroud: The History Press, 2010

Bloom, Clive. *Violent London: 2000 Years of Riots, Rebels and Revolts,* London: Palgrave, 2010

Bunyan, Tony. *The History and Practice of the Political Police in Britain,* London: Quartet, 2010

Burleigh, Michael. *Blood and Rage; a Cultural History of Terrorism,* London: HarperPress, 2008

Cannon, John (Editor). *The Oxford Companion to British History,* Oxford: Oxford, 1997

Chase, Malcolm. *Chartism: A New History,* Manchester: Manchester University Press, 2007

Cook, Chris & Stevenson, John. *The Longman handbook of Modern British History 1714–1980,* Harlow: Longman, 1983

Cowley, Richard. *A History of the British Police; From its Earliest Beginnings to the Present Day,* Stroud: The History Press, 2011

Emsley, Clive. *The Great British Bobby,* London: Quercus, 2009

Evans, Brian. *Bygone Ilford,* Chichester: Phillimore, 1989

Evans, Stewart. *Executioner; the Chronicles of a Victorian Hangman,* Stroud: Sutton Publishing, 2004

Glinert, Ed. *The London Compendium,* London: Allen Lane, 2003

Glinert, Ed. *West End Chronicles,* London: Allen Lane, 2007

Gray, Adrian. *Crime and Criminals of Victorian England,* Stroud: The History Press, 2011

Hamilton, Neil. *Politics Strangest Characters,* London: Robson Books, 2003

Hernon, Ian. *Riot!: Civil Insurrection from Peterloo to the Present Day,* London; Pluto Press, 2006

Jenkins, Brian. *The Fenian Problem; Insurgency and Terrorism in a Liberal State, 1858–1874,* Liverpool: Liverpool University Press, 2009

Jones, Steve. *Capital Punishments,* Nottingham: Wicket Publications, 1992

Lammy, David. *Out of the Ashes; Britain after the Riots,* London: Guardian Books, 2012

Mitchell R.J. & Leys M.D.R. *A History of London Life,* London: Longmans, 1958

Quinlivan, P. & Rose, P. *Fenians in England,* London: Calder Publications, 1983

Sheppard, Francis. *London: a History,* Oxford: Oxford University Press, 1998

Shuckburgh, Julian. *London Revealed,* London: Harper Collins, 2003

Slee, Christopher. *The Guinness Book of Lasts,* Enfield: Guiness Publishing, 1994

Swinnerton, Jo. *The London Companion,* London: Robson Books, 2004

Vallence, Edward. *A Radical History of Britain,* London: Little Brown, 2009

Webb, Simon. *Dynamite, Treason and Plot: Terrorism in Victorian and Edwardian London,* Stroud: The History Press, 2012

Webb, Simon. *Execution: a History of Capital Punishment in Britain,* Stroud: The History Press, 2012

Withington, John. *Capital Disasters,* Stroud: Sutton Publishing, 2003

Index